YOUR FINANCIAL ADVISOR
IS NOT MANAGING YOUR MONEY
(AND NEVER WAS)

YOUR FINANCIAL ADVISOR IS NOT MANAGING YOUR MONEY (AND NEVER WAS)

The Dirty Truth About How Passive Investing Is Failing Millions

JOHN F. REUTEMANN JR., CLU®, CFP®

YOUR FINANCIAL ADVISOR IS NOT MANAGING YOUR MONEY
(AND NEVER WAS)
The Dirty Truth About How Passive Investing Is Failing Millions

ISBN: 978-1-964046-81-5 (Paperback)
        978-1-964046-82-2 (Hardcover)

Expert
Press
www.ExpertPress.net

Editing by Tamma Ford
Copyediting by Hannah Skaggs
Proofreading by Geena Barret
Text design and composition by Emily Fritz
Cover design by Casey Fritz

DEDICATION

When I was asked by my publisher to write a dedication, I knew what it would say immediately.

As I write this, Antoinette Rene Rogan Reutemann and I have been married over fifty-two years, since June 2, 1973. We both graduated from college, then "Toni" went for her Masters in Special Education. We both went to work and made money. That's how it was back then—no living in your parents' basement! After our first of five children was born, my business was doing well enough to allow her to retire from teaching and be a stay-at-home mom. Toni gave me five awesome children. They're all college grads with big jobs. The family boasts two doctors, and our only son is a US Air Force Major chaplain, a Catholic priest with a DMin and an MDiv.

Toni, thank you for fifty-two fabulous years and for our children Kathryn, Colleen, Patricia, John III, and Annaliese. Thank you for Reilly, Jay, and Ben—our terrific sons-in-law—and for our amazing grandchildren Kyra, Landon, Morgan, Macey, Madilynn, Elliott, Nolan, Finnley, and Raegan.

Toni is our family glue. She holds everyone together and accountable. I couldn't have done what I have without her enormous help. In my younger days, there were many twelve-hour days, six days a week. Toni kept it all together. Not one homework assignment was ever missed. Love you forever!

CONTENTS

THE OPENING BELL

Look at this heart-wrenching blast from the past reported on October 19, 1987, by CBS:

> They're calling it the Monday Massacre—the worst drop in Wall Street history. I just came from inside and it looks like a madhouse. . . . By the closing bell, the Dow Jones Industrial Average was in the steepest fall in its 103-year history,[1] down more than 500 points. . . . Today's loss was far greater, more than 22%[2]. . . . more than $500 billion today.[3]

Look at this October 2002 news, even if it still hurts your tech-loving heart:

> The NASDAQ fell from its peak of over 5,000 points in March 2000 to around 1,100 points by

October 2002, a loss of nearly 80% of its value. The market downturn erased about $5 trillion in market value.[4]

Look at this perhaps all-too-familiar 2009 news from the mortgage and financial crash era: During the global financial crisis,[5] the S&P 500 lost nearly 50 percent of its value from its 2007 peak to its 2009 trough, wiping out trillions of dollars in market capitalization worldwide. And on March 5, 2009, the Dow Jones closed at 6,926, a drop of more than 50 percent[6] from its pre-recession high. Note that the above authors and commentators were being generous (or just sloppy in their research and reporting). The bear ended at -57 percent!

If that's not enough to get your blood boiling, all of you are of an age to remember these next two pieces of 2025 news and seethe. On March 14, 2025, CNBC reported:

> The S&P 500's rapid 10% decline from a record high into correction territory has wiped out trillions of dollars in market value. The market value of the S&P 500 at its Feb. 19 peak was $52.06 trillion, according to FactSet. Thursday's decline put the index's market value down to $46.78 trillion. That makes for a total loss of about $5.28 trillion in about three weeks.[7]

And then, on April 3–4, the markets lost $6.6 trillion in value—the largest two-day loss in history, MarketWatch announced.[8] Forbes reported on April 6, 2025, "The U.S. stock market has wiped out $9.6 trillion since Inauguration Day."[9]

But wait!

Market value's down? The market? The S&P lost? The S&P? A loss for the NASDAQ? *The NASDAQ?!*

No, no, no! The market didn't lose. The S&P didn't lose. The NASDAQ didn't lose.

That's the first lie you need to wrap your head around.

It was real, live, flesh-and-blood people who lost.

Real Americans you might know did this losing. They were people like schoolteachers, factory union workers, nurses, electricians, payroll clerks, and mid-level managers. They were big-city, small-town, white-collar, blue-collar, college-educated, trade-school-certified Americans. Let's not forget to add that twenty-eight-year-old granddaughter of yours—the one you encouraged six years ago to sign up for a 401(k) and max it out.

And you. You, your parents, your children, your friends—these flesh-and-blood people lost billions or trillions of dollars, not "the market." Our team at Research Financial Strategies was able to avoid most of the carnage.

S&P 500 index at inflection points

S&P 500 Price Index

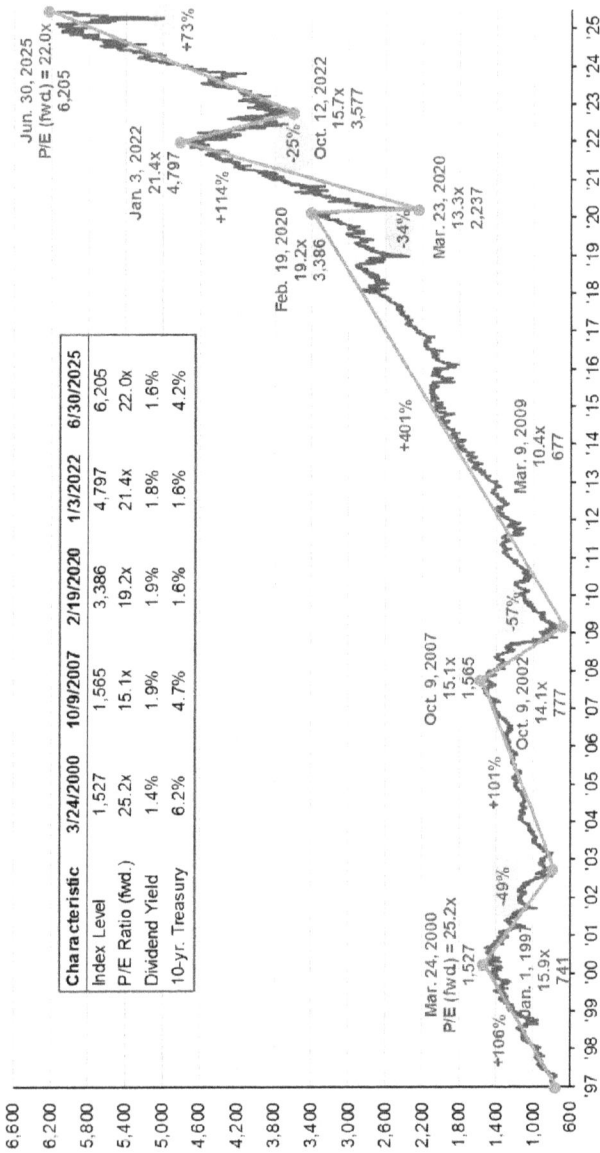

Characteristic	3/24/2000	10/9/2007	2/19/2020	1/3/2022	6/30/2025
Index Level	1,527	1,565	3,386	4,797	6,205
P/E Ratio (fwd.)	25.2x	15.1x	19.2x	21.4x	22.0x
Dividend Yield	1.4%	1.9%	1.9%	1.8%	1.6%
10-yr. Treasury	6.2%	4.7%	1.6%	1.6%	4.2%

Jun. 30, 2025
P/E (fwd.) = 22.0x
6,205

+73%

Jan. 3, 2022
21.4x
4,797

Oct. 12, 2022
15.7x
3,577

-25%

+114%

Feb. 19, 2020
19.2x
3,386

Mar. 23, 2020
13.3x
2,237

-34%

+401%

Mar. 9, 2009
10.4x
677

Oct. 9, 2007
15.1x
1,565

-57%

Oct. 9, 2002
14.1x
777

+101%

Mar. 24, 2000
P/E (fwd.) = 25.2x
1,527

-49%

Jan. 1, 1997
15.9x
741

+106%

6,600
6,200
5,800
5,400
5,000
4,600
4,200
3,800
3,400
3,000
2,600
2,200
1,800
1,400
1,000
600

'97 '98 '99 '00 '01 '02 '03 '04 '05 '06 '07 '08 '09 '10 '11 '12 '13 '14 '15 '16 '17 '18 '19 '20 '21 '22 '23 '24 '25

4

The Page 4 Chart

Say hello to J.P. Morgan's famous "Page 4 Chart." Finance experts all know "Page 4." It is often cited in the financial media. Market analysts often use it for clarity and insight. Historically, it has signaled turning points in the market or major investment themes.

Your investing education begins here. With the Page 4 Chart. This chart, published in J.P. Morgan's monthly "Guide to the Markets,"[1] shows the ups and downs of the S&P 500. (The S&P 500 is a major stock index that tracks the performance of five hundred of the top publicly traded companies in the United States.)

On the opposite page is the Page 4 Chart from June 30, 2025. Later in this book, I will tell you why this chart's highlighted declines in the market are so important to understand—and why the last one has no data. Stay with me! It will all become very clear as we proceed.

U.S. 3Q 2025   As of August 31, 2025

Guide to the Markets

Easily illustrate key investing topics during client conversations.

(To get the most recent version of the Page 4 Chart, just Google "guide to markets." Select the first search result from J.P. Morgan. You will then see this screen. Click through the presentation until you reach Page 4.)

---

1   This chart of the S&P 500 appears in JP Morgan's "Guide to the Markets," published monthly by JP Morgan Asset Management Company. https://am.jpmorgan.com/us/en/asset-management/adv/insights/market-insights/guide-to-the-markets/. This chart is from the June 2025 edition.

Why did union workers, schoolteachers, and your twenty-eight-year-old granddaughter lose that much money in the market? Because of their advisors' buy-and-hold approach to "managing" their accounts. Because their advisors were not, in fact, "managing" their accounts.

I'm going to show you that losing your shirt in a bear market is not inevitable. In fact, it is avoidable.

But first, what kind of market is it where the S&P 500 and the others lose so much of your money?

PART ONE
THOSE KILLER BEARS

Photo credit: iStock.com/jhorrocks

Bears out in the wild kill. So do bear markets.

And yet—*and yet*—most financial advisors don't protect their clients' wealth from those bear attacks.

It's hard enough for most Americans to save any substantial amount of money. And it takes a fair bit of courage to then give that money to a financial advisory firm for management. So it makes me angry that the clients of those firms are not getting the money management services they pay for.

Let's look at what makes a bear market. I'll reveal to you what no one else wants you to know. I'll reveal the fallout of a bear market for so many people. I'll talk about what those financial advisors are or aren't doing to protect your investments.

Only then can we examine how to beat the bear—and protect your wealth.

1
BEARS ARE KILLERS.
SO ARE BEAR MARKETS.

A stock market chart, called the Page 4 Chart, opens this book. Go back to page 4 and look at it. It shows the Standard & Poor's 500 index (S&P 500). You see that the line from left to right rises and falls. It's pretty straightforward as far as charts go.

What Is a Bear Market?

Everyone who's ever invested money knows that a rising line indicates a bull market and rising prices. This is when everyone's getting greedy, pouring more money into the markets because they're making money. Everyone is strutting their stuff because they feel so smart.

When the line makes a large descent, it's called a bear market, and prices are falling. It's also when everyone's panicking, scared to death, wringing their hands, and finally just getting the hell out of Dodge. How? They pull their money out of the market at the worst time to sell.

I'll come back to that chart in just a minute. It's a chart of the S&P 500 index, as I said, or the top 500 companies listed on the stock exchange. While it's not the only index and chart out there (more on that later), it is one of the most commonly consulted.

Most people don't know that the S&P 500 wasn't born until 1957. If you want to accurately quote the S&P 500 with maximum data, that's the year to start.

However, a respected firm called Yardeni Research has gone back into historic records and compiled data[10] showing that since 1925, we've had twenty-two bear markets. Count that as ninety-nine years of data becuase 2025 isn't over yet.

The official definition of a bear market is **more than a 20 percent drop in value**. If the market declines 19.99 percent, it's not officially counted as a bear market (and that's why my Page 4 Chart shows no negative percentage data in that June 2025 drop—because it didn't drop more than 20 percent). Expand that definition, however, and there have been another 150 of those bear markets since 1925.

What I find interesting is that the public isn't being told this historic truth. If you divide ninety-nine years by twenty-two bear markets, we could theoretically **expect a bear market every 4.7 years**. That's theory. In reality, they could also come more frequently than that.

Let's say the American adult works and saves for more than forty years. That would theoretically mean every one of us would experience eight or so bear markets. And that's just counting the "official" bear markets. You simply must factor in those other drops in the market that come in at 19.99 percent or less.

The question is not whether we'll have more bear markets. It's how we can weather them without losing our shirts.

As a father of five and a grandfather of nine, I'm scared.

A lot of young people are just getting to the point where they can afford to start a 401(k) or begin saving some discretionary income. What scares me most is the number of people invested in the stock market who are (probably like those young people) investing novices. They don't know much, if anything, about the financial markets. I worry about all those who are median earners while being great savers or investors. A median earner/saver arriving at retirement can't afford a bear market—and they're not the only ones.

Reading the J.P. Morgan Page 4 Chart

Turn back to the Page 4 Chart. In the industry, it's so famous and so referenced that we all just call it "Page 4."

The reason Page 4 is so powerful is that it doesn't say "Jack Reutemann's Guide to the Markets." It's not my chart, so you can't say I'm inventing anything. It's the J.P. Morgan "Guide to the Markets," and it's free to anyone who wants it over the internet. The guide is a detailed document of many, many pages and lots of technical language. I've pointed out only one page of it, the S&P 500 chart that always appears on its fourth page.

The chart pinpoints each top (high point) by the S&P 500 value and the percentage gain, a +x number, from the prior bottom. It then details each bottom (low point) to two decimal places, the date, and the percentage drop (you'll see a -x number).

You can see that from March 2000 to October 2002 on the Page 4 Chart, there was a bear market. The so-called dot-com bubble burst and went splat to the tune of 49 percent of the index's value.

Fast-forward a mere four years (less than the historic average) to 2007, and you see another drop on the chart all the way to 2009. This loss of 57 percent was commonly called the Mortgage and Financial Crisis or the Great Recession.

That 57 percent loss equaled $11 trillion, which evaporated in seventeen months. Again, I want you to know my position: "The markets" did not lose. Real people lost $11 trillion.

An individual investor with, for example, $200,000 in the markets found himself with only $86,000 after this debacle. What would you do if you lost $114,000?

If you are someone who has saved more than that, add a zero to feel the pain. If you had $2,000,000 in the markets, would you be happy if your advisor lost $1,140,000 of *your money?*

I think not.

Now you might be asking this: "If someone lost everything in the dot-com bubble bear market of 2000, did they have enough time to make back their losses before the next bear market hit in 2007–09?" I'll address that soon. Stay with me, and let's keep looking at that Page 4 Chart.

Move to the right on the chart to 2020, and you see what happened in February 2020. Another bear attack. In one month, the index dropped 34 percent. It blindsided a lot of investors.

The numbers took two years to come back to pre-February levels, only to decline again. The S&P 500 dropped 25 percent between January and October 2022. You could say the pandemic years were hard on investors because that 4.7-year average between bear markets got compressed.

You've looked at January 1 to March 23, 2020, which was -34 percent. I didn't say that; J.P. Morgan did after looking at the data. You see that from October 2007 to March 2009 was -57 percent. I didn't say that. The data said it. It's the statistical history of bear markets.

Bear Markets Really Hurt

Let me sum it up (using data as of July 14, 2025):

- The average depth of a bear market is a **37.31 percent decline**.
- The average duration of a bear market is **15.74 months**.
- The average time lost making up a bear market loss is **59 months**.
- All new growth occurred in just **34 percent** of the time period.

- In sixty-three of ninety-five years (**66 percent of the time**), people were just putting their own money back in their pockets.

"Putting your own money back in your pocket" is not why you invested. You don't want to end up with only the capital you put in. That wasn't the point, was it?

The Stakes

Let me make you really squirm. There's a phenomenon called "sequence-of-returns risk." We'll start with some examples of how it can affect you, and I'll go deeper into how it works later.

If you were sixty-five years old when you retired in March 2000, you walked into a 49 percent decline in your portfolio value. It took the S&P 500 index seven years and two months to recover to its pre-bear-market peak. By that time, you were seventy-two years old. You might have depleted your portfolio just to cover your expenses over those seven-plus years. You might have outright canceled all your early retirement overseas adventures, thinking that now you wouldn't have the funds. You caught yourself hoping and praying the market would go back up again—and faster, please! And if you were extremely nervous, you might have further compounded your market loss by depleting your individual retirement account (IRA) and incurring withdrawal penalties.

It would have taken eighty-two months, or 6.8 years, for your portfolio to break even at a 10 percent investment return per year. But, not all advisors put you in such investments. What if you were earning only a 5 percent return per year? It would have taken you 161 months to break even, or nearly 13.5 years. You'd have turned seventy-nine years old before you got back the money you had lost.

This sequence of returns was not in your favor. Quite the contrary. And what sixty-five-year-old has that kind of time? It's panic-inducing for far too many investors, and that pisses me off. Not that *the advisors* are panicked—oh, no. What makes me angry is that they lost the money in the first place.

In my opinion as a professional, the devastating losses of all those people's hard-earned money is right on the advisors' heads. I'll be ranting about that in the next chapters, but just let me explain why I feel justified in blaming your advisor—even though I'm an advisor too.

It's Possible to Beat the Bear

At my firm, Research Financial Strategies (RFS), we're not like other advisors. We've beaten the bear for most of the thirty-three years we've been serving investors. That didn't happen by chance or by luck. We have strategies to achieve that.

In each of the bear markets we just saw in the Page 4 Chart, my team and I achieved the results in table 1 for our clients. It's because we do things differently from those other advisors.

Table 1. Bear Market Performance: RFS vs. S&P 500 (2000–22)

The Bear	The S&P 500	My Firm, RFS
2000–02 dot-com crash	-49%	+13%
2007–09 mortgage & financial crisis	-57%	-4%
2020 pandemic	-34%	-1%
2022 bear market	-25%	-5%

Yes, my firm was in the single-digit negatives in three of those markets. But look at how small those losses are compared to the index's losses. Our clients were much better off—our numbers were nowhere near as painful as those suffered by most advisors' client accounts.

I'm not writing this book on technical analysis (maybe the next book can be about that). I'm not writing a book on reading charts filled with advanced data. My goal isn't to teach you how to do any of that. I'm not getting into that very much at all. But, I'll do it just enough for you to understand that your advisor is lying to you.

To get the results my firm gets, it takes ten to fifteen of our staff staring at the computer from 9:30 a.m. to 4 p.m. every day. On any given day, our team is analyzing over three thousand stocks, bonds, and exchange-traded funds (ETFs).

We are *active* managers in my firm. We'll know when your growth stocks might be eaten by the bear. It's our job to know when the market is going up and it's your turn to eat the bear.

As my numbers show, we don't let our clients' wealth be devoured by a bear market decline like everyone else does. We take the necessary steps to protect your wealth. That, as we see it, is as much our job as increasing your wealth.

How do I dare say that everyone else in my industry sits there watching the bear? How do I dare say they're not serving your very best interests? Well, if the hundreds of thousands of advisors in this country did their jobs, you wouldn't be afraid of putting your hard-earned $250,000 into the markets.

Look at the chart. It tells the whole story.

I don't care what your political beliefs are. I have to say this, though. After the 2024 election, James Carville wrote, "Perception is everything in politics, and a lot of Americans perceive Democrats as *not feeling their pain or caring too much about other issues.* If we're going to win again, we've got to *show people that we understand what they're going through and that we have their backs*" (italics mine).[11] Mr. Carville is a Democratic Party critic, and no doubt just one among many, but he's made a point. The point, in my opinion, applies to the financial services industry. Failing to demonstrate care for their clients is what financial advisors have been doing for decades and decades. They're looking after themselves, not you. They don't have your back. Ever heard the famous Wall Street joke: "Where are all the customers' yachts?"

It makes me angry. I'm really upset with those financial advisors who aren't managing anything for you. I'm pissed that they're giving us all a bad name. I'm angry that they won't do their jobs for their clients in spite of having all the information, tools, and resources that my team and I use. I'll have a lot more to say about them in the rest of these pages.

I am also deeply distressed about the untold side of the story.

Yes, a market decline of 57 percent is staggering. But what many fail to grasp is the collateral damage. Unless you dive into the statistics (I'm a technical market analyst, so I do), you won't know the effects a 57 percent decline has on an investor. Unless you talk with mental health professionals (and I have some among my clients, so I do), you don't know what investors are going through in such a bear market.

Psychologists Know

What keeps me up at night is the darker side of bear markets. Some of it may leak into media reports, but the media don't really like to broadcast it. What I'm about to tell you isn't on the website of any major financial advisory or brokerage firms, but that doesn't make it any less true.

I can tell you firsthand about it. Among my clients, I have well over twenty practicing psychiatrists, psychologists, social workers, and other mental health professionals who talk and fret about this.

Remember what happened in 2009, the -57 percent bear market? That was a deep recession period. It was also the year that suicides, medical depression, alcohol and drug abuse, and cases of domestic violence all went through the roof.

By the summer of 2009, the mental health profession was sounding the alarm, and not just in the US. *The British Journal of Psychiatry*[12] reported on the suicide rates of that year, estimating that the economic crisis in Europe and North America led to more than 10,000 extra suicides. Forbes picked up[13] and reported on the study's findings, as did the BBC.[14]

So the dark side to -57 percent isn't on any financial services website, which might only say, "Oops, sorry! You lost 57 percent of your money. Just stay the course. Hold on, and the market will bounce back."

I have a home in Florida, but I'm from Montgomery County, Maryland. It's one of the most affluent counties in the nation (maybe because Washington, DC, is on its border).

This is where all the big corporations and many large federal agencies are located. We have Marriott International, Lockheed Martin, the US Food & Drug Administration (FDA), the US National Institutes of Health (NIH), the US Department of Health & Human Services (HHS), Bethesda Naval/Walter Reed Medical Center, Montgomery County Public Schools (one of the largest school districts in the United States with over two hundred schools),

Giant-Landover Foods, Adventist Healthcare, Johns Hopkins Medicine, and so on.

It's also where many wealthy doctors, lawyers, businesspeople, and Congress members call home. They want their kids in Montgomery County's outstanding schools.

Why would I tell you this? Not to brag. Nope. To give you context.

I have a client, Dr. M. He's seventy-eight years old this year and is still a practicing psychologist. He could have afforded to retire twenty years ago, but he loves his work. A few months back (early spring 2025), he said to me, "Jack, I'm getting burned out. I'm working six days a week, eleven hours a day, seeing sixty-six patients every week, and I have a waiting list of sixty more people trying to get in to see me."

I was shocked. "Doc, you're in the middle of one of the richest counties in the nation. How can there be that many people in Montgomery County, Maryland, who need you?"

He sighed. "A lot of people in Montgomery County, Maryland—a hell of a lot—are in trouble. In some cases, it's unemployment. In some cases, it's couples working ten to eleven hours a day, and their marriages are falling apart."

As the bear markets hit, we as a nation witness alarming spikes in suicide, depression, domestic abuse, violence, substance abuse, foreclosures, evictions, and repossessions. This is what I've been calling "bear market collateral damage."

The good doctor wouldn't reveal more to me. He's a mental health therapist in one of the richest counties in the nation, but the number of people in some kind of mental, emotional, or monetary pain there is beyond believable. It's due to bear markets decimating their wealth and having a ripple effect on so many other areas of their lives.

Right alongside this, we have many college graduates out there who are working for the most part, sure, yet still living with their parents. Their annual college tuition was more than any job is now offering them. We live in a mad, crazy world.

No big financial advisory firms talk about this. Nothing I just told you is on their websites. All that's on those websites is rubbish like "We're bullish" and "You can't time the market." They want you to do that buy-and-hold thing. They want you to stay in the game for the long term.

James Carville and others may have been right that the Democrats don't care too much about Americans. However, in my view, they pointed their fingers at the wrong people. Financial advisors weren't even on their radar. The big brokerage firms and their so-called advisors abandoned you too. You got no management. As a result, you were down 57 percent.

It's a grim reality that "the markets" are not the losers. Investors are. They risk their wealth, their emotional and physical health, their marriages, and their homes. Younger people are depressed by never being able to afford a home or save money, much less keep up with student loan debt.

This crisis scenario is cleverly denied and obscured by the buy-and-hold, wait-it-out narrative of the big firms.

I'm going to reveal what's really going on because almost no investors know. And you must.

2
THE MAULING

We saw it in chapter 1: While investors are pleased at a rising bull market, they panic when a bear market hits. The majority of financial advisory firms and their personnel are part of the panic problem.

If we're having a bull market, everybody's money is gaining—boats all rise together. In a bull market, my firm doesn't look much different from others in the industry.

My particular business does best in volatile bear markets. This is because my firm looks and acts differently from other firms and their advisors. In any bear market correction—*any of* them—we apply a formula that the others ignore.

We use a "sell-side strategy" (more on that later). It allowed us and our clients to be down by only 1 percent when the next-to-last bear market, according to the S&P 500 data, was down 34 percent.

Me? I'm happy to have this strategy and to apply it for my clients with success. In my opinion, those other advisors who have the same tools as my team but don't use them are incompetent. They're not money managers. Far from it. They are the problem.

I do know this: If I can contribute to fixing the problem, then that's part of my agenda. If I can be part of the solution with this book and the knowledge you gain from it, I will have achieved my goal.

History Repeats Itself

Human beings in general, and Americans in particular, are lousy historians. Just look at World Wars I and II, the Korean conflict, Vietnam, Afghanistan, and Iraq. It just keeps going on and on. We just keep marching off to war because some baked-in institution (that can't see the world differently) says so.

As I showed you in chapter 1, the financial markets in our country have lots of history. There is lots of data to learn from, trends to analyze, and patterns to understand and use to our advantage.

Most advisors don't do any of that for their clients' benefit.

Americans—not just advisors—are notoriously guilty of not learning from history. And that's a problem when you're trying to understand today's problems (which might just be history repeating itself). Learn from history if you really want to get ahead.

In the stock markets, we have lots and lots of history. Most are not learning from it. I resent that. As a professional, I learn. I educate my clients and advise them of risks. I tell them our strategy to avoid or mitigate risks to their wealth. Stay with me, and you'll learn too.

Who's Managing Your Risk?

When skies are blue, employment is strong, and times are good, Americans don't focus on risk management. After all, you don't need car insurance when your vehicle is parked safely in the garage. You don't need flood protection for your house till the drought ends and water starts rising around it.

It's the old joke that in a bull market, the sun is always shining, and no one who owns trailer parks is lined up to buy hurricane insurance.

But when the bears attack, that's exactly like when the hurricane is three miles off the coast. People mob Geico and State Farm hotlines and agent offices and try to get hurricane insurance. And the insurance companies' answer is "Of course you can't. Are you stupid? You should have called us when the sun was shining and the sky was blue."

The same thing happens in a bear market. Unfortunately, this is a good analogy for the majority of Americans with money invested or to invest. They don't understand risk management because it's not on their radar when all markets are rising. And when the bear attacks, they haven't managed their risk, but neither have their advisors.

In our history of stock markets, we have had bear markets. The question is, do you understand the implications of a bear market for you and your life? Bear markets affect your salary and your health. They affect your marriage, your kids' ability to go to college, and your ability to pay the mortgage.

In 2007–09, millions of people walked away from their homes. The common phrase then was "We're underwater," meaning the equity in their homes had disappeared, and they were drowning in mortgage payments and other bills, unable to hang onto the house any longer. There were millions of foreclosures and short sales.

Table 2 summarizes the nationwide US foreclosure filings in all stages (default notices, auction sale notices, bank repossessions, etc.) during and just after the Great Recession.[15]

Table 2. Foreclosures, 2007–12

Year	Total Foreclosure Filings, All Stages	Properties Affected When Known
2007	~ 1,800,000	1,283,943
2008	3,157,806	2,330,483
2009	3,957,643	2,824,674
2010	~ 2,900,000	
2011	~ 2,300,000	
2012	2,304,941	1,836,634

Add up the foreclosures in the table. Go ahead. It's the largest number in our history in such a time frame. There were 16,420,390 foreclosures according to the data I found (and note that the industry, or at least some data gatherers, seem to have only rounded the numbers for 2007, 2010, and 2011).

More than that, we must remember that loss of a significant asset and symbol of security such as a home is devastating, not just financially but emotionally, to any property owner and their household. Mental health studies associate suicides with those foreclosures.[16] Real people took their lives. Add that to what we said previously about bear market losses, recession, and the mental health ramifications. It's the personal fallout that is the most devastating, and it breaks my heart that our nation came to this place.

Imagine you and your spouse lose 40 percent of your retirement funds. Do you understand the consequences of that?

I'd put my hand in the fire and say that your employer's 401(k) administrator has never, ever talked about bear markets. The administrator also never uttered the words "market risk," "potential for loss," or "protective strategies" to you.

That's what makes me angry. It's not just that these financial advisors—so-called professional money managers—are not really managing your gains optimally in bull markets. They're also putting their heads in the sand about what happens to your wealth when the bear comes barreling along.

This approach, this attitude toward money, is all the more surprising because the wealthiest 1 percent of

Americans control a majority of shares in the US stock market. Wouldn't you think they'd be the smart ones? Wouldn't you think they'd want their advisors to protect and grow that great wealth? It's a question for the ages!

Don't believe me? Look at figure 1.[17] The wealthiest 1 percent of individuals own half of all corporate equities and mutual funds[18] in the United States, per the St. Louis Federal Reserve. The top 10 percent of Americans by wealth own close to 90 percent of all stock market holdings. What's also telling is that this ownership hasn't changed meaningfully over time. They've owned 80–90 percent since the end of the 1980s.

Figure 1. Who Owns Stocks in the United States

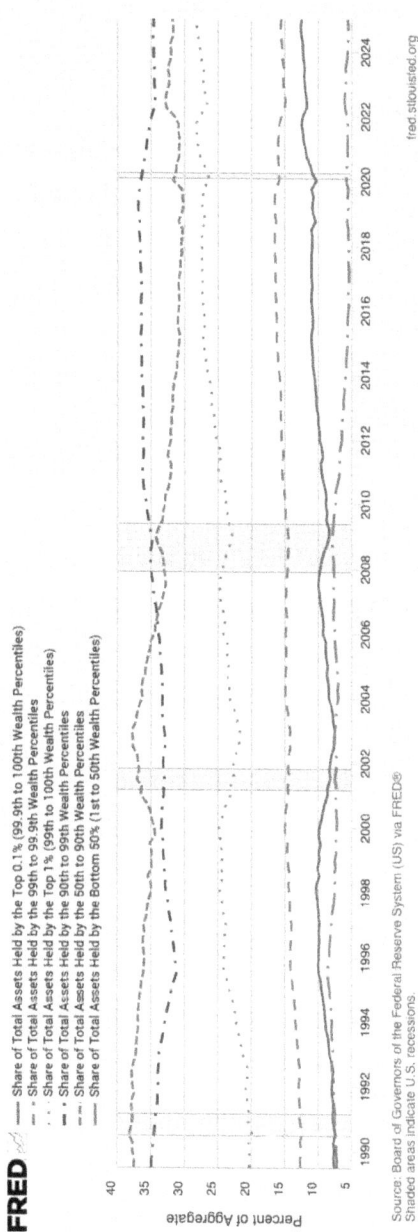

Source: Board of Governors of the Federal Reserve System (US) via FRED®
Shaded areas indicate U.S. recessions.

Most Americans Have Debt, Not Wealth

What about the flip side of that coin? If the top 10 percent own 90 percent of all stock holdings, what about the rest of our population?

Well, 77 percent of our population owes money. According to the American Public Health Association, in 2019, 77 percent of US households reported holding some type of debt.[19] That's three out of four people, households, and families with debt instead of wealth.

That includes not only credit card debt, which is $1.21 trillion[20] in 2025 all on its own. It's also mortgages and home equity lines of credit (HELOCs), auto loans, and student loans. It's personal loans, medical debt, legal financial obligations like child support, and so on. We're in debt not just for wants but for needs like housing and healthcare.

Out-of-pocket medical costs are already known to decimate too many Americans' wealth and savings. Those out-of-pocket costs could be tens of thousands or hundreds of thousands of dollars. I can't fix the health insurance industry, but please recognize that the loss in a bear market is not very different. It could be devastatingly worse.

None of this is the sign of the "greatest economy in the world," as some of our politicians brag. It's not the affluence we grow up hoping for, expecting, and deserving. It's not the American Dream.

National Debt Is Personal Debt

Not everyone is comfortable carrying debt even though it might be a necessity. People tell me, "I don't feel rich with debt, but once it's paid off, I feel free!"

We know that 52–64 percent of the public is living paycheck to paycheck,[21] and at the end of the month, many have more debt than they have income to pay the debt. Up to two-thirds of credit card holders don't or can't pay off their balance in full every month. They are counting on next month's income to get by now. (These numbers vary,[22] as institutions in the industry have their own data, but you get the idea).

Those paycheck-to-paycheck people are called "non-discretionary consumers." They don't have the money to go to Home Depot and buy materials for a $50,000 home renovation. The remainder of the people are "discretionary consumers." They pay all their bills on time and have no rollover in their credit card balances. They have money left over after paying their bills and other expenses.

The charts my team and I use tell us whether people who have money—the discretionary consumers—are or are not spending it. This group will spend in a bull market like they're doing today, in mid 2025. But, in bear markets, they won't spend it. They sit on their cash and wait (see my chapter on the Eleven Charts for more detail about why).

This isn't just my opinion. Home Depot's chief financial officer (CFO), Richard McPhail, appeared on CNBC on August 13, 2024, to discuss how business looked for the company.[23] This was, of course, before the 2024 presidential election.

One of the reporters said it didn't look like Home Depot was having a great year.

The CFO said, "Let me tell you what our partners are telling us."

To understand his response, you have to know who Home Depot's partners are. They are all the professional construction companies and general contractors that buy materials to build for other people. You and I, the retail shopper, are not their partners.

The CFO reports that the company's partners see that rich people aren't spending money. It isn't because they don't have it or because they're afraid of the interest rates. Home Depot's partners are telling them that rich people aren't spending money *because of fear*.

Banks hoard cash. So do wealthy individuals. The banks stop lending. The rich stop spending. They're scared of the future and scared to lend and spend. Banks and the rich hate uncertainty.

I made a big note of that for my team at the time: They're not lending or spending money because they're scared.

Back to the Bear

Let's extrapolate. If the bulk of the population holds over a trillion dollars in credit card debt and doesn't have enough discretionary income to pay it off, how likely are they to have significant liquidity for investments or 401(k) deposits? How likely is it that they've been saving (or that they've been able to save) for their retirement?

Not very likely.

I don't hide this: I work with affluent clients. But, I'm no fool. I know that Americans between ages sixty-five and seventy-four have an average of $200,000[24] in savings. Because that's an average, many Americans will scoff and say, "Jack, please. We have less. *Far* less." Then we have those who've been saving so much more and who are so affluent, they get to use investment advisors and certified financial planners.

I have a very good friend who's an extreme liberal. He said to me one day, "Jack, how could you complain about Biden's administration when your real estate and stock market net worth probably doubled during his four-year term?"

I immediately responded, "Because my net worth is not the problem. What about the 77 percent in our country whose net worth didn't double because they're broke and they're sharing that $1.21 trillion in credit card debt? Even the value of their primary residence has crashed."

At the end of the day, America is not much different from any country you could name: We've got some extreme poverty alongside some extreme wealth. Are we going to allow ourselves to always have two Americas, the extremely rich and the extremely poor? I don't think that bodes well for what could happen down the road. I think if we go back through the ages and study countries that have fallen apart, it all has something to do with the ultra-wealthy and the ultra-poor trying to coexist.

Okay, my worried, angry rant is over (for now). Back to you with money in the markets. Back to saving for retirement or for a grandchild's college.

When will you need your money? I'm talking about the money you invested with an advisor that got decimated by the most recent bear market.

Do You Have Time to Recover After a Bear Market?

The stock market is a giant swimming pool. There are people getting in and people getting out every day.

If you turned sixty-five and retired on October 9, 2007 (and we can be sure thousands of people did), you immediately walked into a -57 percent bear market, as I discussed in chapter 1. You got mauled. The day you retired, you walked into 57 percent less wealth than you thought you had. Your sequence-of-returns risk came true.

You planned on getting out of the world of work and using your accumulated wealth to enjoy retirement. And you got clobbered by -57 percent or some other devastating amount of loss.

When this happens, as I've mentioned, it can take time to get back to the amount you had (not to mention starting to profit again). But how much time does it take to break even after a bear attack? You guessed it:

1. It depends.
2. Too long.

Let's learn from history why you absolutely want an advisor with a bear-protective strategy.

The major bear markets of the past century appear in table 3. As you examine them, you might think, "Well, I have 3, 7, 22, or 25 months of ready cash to wait until I've broken even." Maybe. Keep reading the chart. Do you really have 302 months—twenty-five years—of cash reserves to tide you over while you wait, wait, and wait some more to gain back what you lost? Especially if you're sixty-five years old when those months begin?

Also think about the fact that your investments are not gaining anything in all of those months. You're just playing catch-up.

Look at the tables below that my team has collated. You'll have to wait for my Scary Math Chapter to know how I calculated those break-even or recovery times. Shake in your boots right now, imagining that *you retire a couple of days before* one of those bears attacks. Let's start with table 3, which shows the performance of the S&P 500.

Table 3. S&P 500 Time to Break Even After Bear Markets, 1929–2002

Bear Market	Duration	S&P 500 Decline	Time to Break Even
September 1929–June 1932	33 months	-86.70%	302 months
July 1933–March 1935	20 months	-33.90%	28 months
March 1937–March 1938	12 months	-54.50%	107 months
November 1938–April 1942	41 months	-45.80%	77 months
May 1946–March 1948	22 months	-28.10%	49 months
August 1956–October 1957	14 months	-21.60%	25 months
December 1961–June 1962	6 months	-28.00%	22 months
February 1966–October 1966	8 months	-22.20%	16 months
November 1968–May 1970	18 months	-36.10%	39 months
January 1973–October 1974	21 months	-48.20%	91 months

Bear Market	Duration	S&P 500 Decline	Time to Break Even
November 1980– August 1982	21 months	-27.10%	25 months
August 1987– December 1987	3 months	-33.50%	23 months
July 1990– October 1990	3 months	-19.90%	7 months
July 1998– October 1998	3 months	-21.20%	3 months
March 2000– October 2002	31 months	-49.10%	87 months

Don't get sassy too fast when you can say, "I'll be *fine*—I own only blue chip stocks." Table 4 shows what your wait could look like by looking at what happened after the dot-com bubble burst and the Great Recession.

Table 4. Large Corporations' Time to Break Even After Twenty-First-Century Crashes

Dow Component	2000-02 Performance	Back to Even
Coca-Cola	-45%	2011
General Electric	-63%	Unknown
Altria	-67%	2005
Disney	-68%	2011
Merck	-59%	2007
Walmart	-40%	2012
Exxon	-36%	2004

Dow Component	2000-02 Performance	Back to Even
Alcoa	-60%	2007
Home Depot	-70%	2013
Hewlett Packard	-84%	Unknown
AT&T	-67%	2016
Microsoft	-65%	2015

Dow Component	10/9/07–3/9/09 Performance	Back to Even
Coca-Cola	-33%	2010
General Electric	-82%	Unknown
Altria	-26%	2010
Disney	-56%	2010
Merck	-61%	2014
Walmart	-5%	2008
Exxon	-30%	2013
Alcoa	-86%	Unknown
Home Depot	-46%	2010
Hewlett Packard	-51%	2010
AT&T	-48%	2016
Microsoft	-50%	2009

Let me call you up short again if you tell me, "I'm in diversified mutual funds. Diversification means I can't get hurt." Let me burst your bubble with table 5.

Table 5. Mutual Funds' Time to Break Even After Twenty-First-Century Bear Markets

Mutual Fund	2000–02 Performance	Back to Even
Fidelity Magellan	-49%	2007
Vanguard 500 Index	-46%	2006
Washington Mutual	-29%	2004
Fidelity Growth and Inc.	-36%	2006
Investment Co. of America	-29%	2004
Fidelity Contrafund	-35%	2005
Vanguard Windsor II	-33%	2005
Fidelity Growth Opps	-53%	2007
Vanguard Wellington	-19%	2004

Mutual Fund	10/9/07–3/9/09 Performance	Back to Even
American Funds Growth	-52%	2013
American Funds Cap Inc	-43%	2013
Fidelity Contrafund	-48%	2012
American Funds Cap World	-52%	2009
Vanguard Total Stock	-55%	2013
American Funds Inv Co Amer	-51%	2013
American Funds Income	-45%	2014

Mutual Fund	10/9/07–3/9/09 Performance	Back to Even
Vanguard 500 Index	-55%	2013
American Funds Washington	-54%	2013
Vanguard Inst Index	-55%	2013

I won't include charts for the remaining bear markets, but just know that they ended, respectively, at these points:

- -34 percent on March 23, 2020
- -25 percent on October 12, 2022
- -19 percent on April 8, 2025 (not quite a bear but a close call)

All the above historical data shows what really happened. It does take a long time to recover losses. Most people lack either the time or the patience to wait. I think you get the idea that a bear market will eat your wealth down to nothing without action. Only when you've broken even can you start to make gains and profits again.

But not everyone gets math. I know this because I hear, "Jack, why so long to break even?" Math. When you're down 40 percent, it doesn't just take a gain of 40 percent to break even. Have a look at my team's math in figure 2, and understand better why it takes a while to reach pre-bear levels.

Figure 2. Gain Required to Fully Recover from a Loss

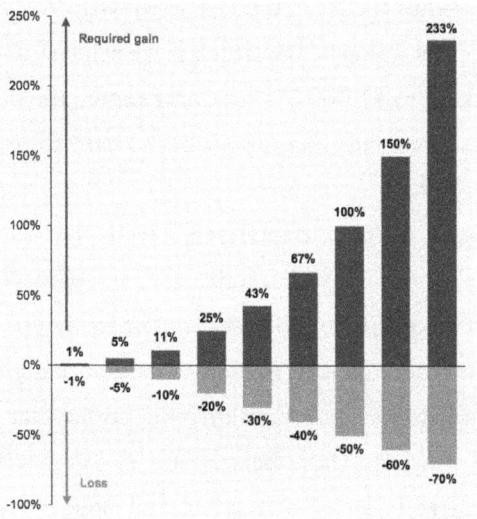

Source: Pieter, "50 Investing Visuals," *Compounding Quality* (blog), accessed August 26, 2025, https://www.compoundingquality.net/p/resources.

When you suffer a loss in an investment, recovering is a process of taking two steps back and one step forward. Look at the middle of the chart, where it shows you need to earn 43 percent to break even after a 30 percent loss. Why do you have to make so much more?

Let's use some concrete numbers to illustrate it. Say you invest $1,000, and the market tanks. You lose 30 percent of that, so now you have only $700.

You might think you just need the investment to earn 30 percent again, and you'll be whole. But 30 percent of

$700 is $210, so if it earns that percentage, you'll still have only $910—not the $1,000 you started with. You need that $700 to earn another $300, which is 43 percent, to bring its value back up to $1,000. As the chart shows, the deeper the losses, the more your investment has to earn to recover the value it once had.

None of us has a crystal ball. Maybe you know when you'll need your money after retirement and why. Maybe you don't. But wouldn't it be better for your money to be there all the time because you had advisors who paid attention to the markets for you? Wouldn't you be happier if they'd protected you from those bears? Sure, but that would have required them to let go of the buy-and-hold narrative and use a strategy that actually works.

3

THE BUY-AND-HOLD INSANITY

If you're wondering how anyone loses 57 percent of their portfolio's value in a bear market, it's due to an advisor's approach called buy-and-hold.

Whenever I sit with a prospective client, I make no assumptions about their investing or stock market know-how. I appreciate that they come to us for our knowledge and expertise. They just don't want to face that steep learning curve themselves.

Here, too, I won't assume you know what buy-and-hold even means. I'll be talking about it a lot, so here goes.

Buy-and-hold is a passive investment strategy. Your money is invested for the long term. It's presumably in very sound vehicles (stocks, etc.), with the intention of holding onto all your positions through any ups and downs, and through any volatility and market fluctuations. The primary rule is if the market trends downward, you don't sell. You ride out the downturn. You sit and wait for it to turn around and rise again.

Do you hold forever? Often, with many, many advisors. But not always. The theory is that the market always bounces back and that you'll break even (eventually) and start to profit again. The rule of buy-and-hold has two parts:

1. Aim for long-term growth of your holdings.
2. Never try to time market highs or lows.

Well, you saw the chapter 2 tables. You know now how long bouncing back might just take. Too long!

Advisors and investment houses in favor of buy-and-hold (because that's all they do) will attack anyone using data to drive their investment decisions. "You're just trying to time the markets," they accuse.

They tout the value of patience.[25] What they really mean is, "Just sit on your investments; let's just stick with our buy-and-hold approach." You can read those words almost any day of the year in the financial media. However, the proponents of buy-and-hold seem to come out of the woodwork in defense of this passive strategy more often in volatile times. Why? This is when their clients are nervous about losing their shirts. They must retain those clients at all costs.

Go to any brokerage firm website. Read any finance writer's blogs. Listen to any financial television show's talking heads. You'll hear (and at the oddest times):

- "We're bullish."
- "The markets always bounce back."
- "The end of the correction is in sight."
- "The market always goes higher and higher."

All these phrases are code for buy-and-hold. Advisors who advocate this strategy, such as Burton Malkiel, who wrote *A Random Walk Down Wall Street: The Time-Tested Strategy for Successful Investing*, don't like impatient investors who want out, even if it's to protect their wealth. They tell their clients, "There's a risk if you don't hold on." That risk is missing "the majority of the best ten days"[26] to make up your losses. Those ten days typically occur within two weeks of the worst ten days, making timing the market nearly impossible to execute effectively. Or so they say. (I'll have more to say about this ridiculous ten-days theory in a later chapter).

One article on ETF.com from May 15, 2025, discusses the S&P 500's drop of "nearly 20 percent" from this year's February high. It states that "the index clawed back into positive territory for the year—marking one of the swiftest market recoveries in decades." It only "flirted with a bear market" (defined, as you recall, as a 20 percent or more decline), and wasn't it great that the market bounced back up so quickly?

Now, how were they going to know the market would bounce back as fast as it did? They could point to market confusion due to President Trump's on and off tariff threats, but they couldn't have any idea how the market would react going forward. They just said they don't believe in the value of market timing. If they managed their clients' portfolios with data-driven tools—and at least 89 percent of advisors don't seem to, and more on that in a few pages—they'd have seen the technical indicators foreshadowing that decline. Maybe they saw them, and maybe they didn't. They certainly took no action for their clients if they did.

Then there's the belief that news stories, such as the April 6, 2025, announcement of Trump's tariff deadline, are what cause the market to go down. Advisors and talking heads, on the one hand, blame Trump for the downward move in the market. On the other hand, they reassure everyone with, "Oh no, don't worry, it's just a piece of news. Wait it out. The market will bounce back. It always does." In other words, "Buy and hold, folks. This is just a passing thing."

Similarly, if there's a big CEO scandal, that company's stock plummets, but commentators state (as if they have a crystal ball), "Oh, that scandal's to blame. But once their board of directors puts a new CEO in place, the stock price will bounce back. It's just a passing thing. Wait it out, folks, and you'll be fine."

In my mind, these are not data-driven events or statements. Historically—and in the very big picture of the S&P 500's total context—it's true that the market bounces back and keeps rising. The S&P 500 is higher today than it was back in 1957, when "official" tracking started. So, generally speaking, it's a true statement.

So what's the problem? There are two.

First, no one is saying there's any sort of legal guarantee that the S&P 500 will recover. There isn't. They're wishing and hoping. And right now, in June 2025, the S&P 500 is below its February 16, 2025, high, but it's higher than it was in 1957. So the S&P 500 is higher than it was in 1957, but may not be higher than your most recent bear market losses.

Frankly, when your 2025 money is on the line, do you care about 1957?

What news broadcasts are not telling you is the true financial as well as real human damage from the bear markets. Real investors are getting turned upside down and inside out. That in itself makes me angry. But their advisors are shrugging and saying, "Buy-and-hold, folks." That's denial. That's like a sin of omission. Personally? I think it's a crime. And it pisses me off!

These two phenomena combined are like saying, "I got in a really bad car accident. I was in intensive care for a year, part of which I was in a coma. Then I was in physical therapy for seven years. But now? Hey, I'm perfectly fine! So because I'm 100 percent better, let's pretend the car accident never happened."

Bull crap. Bear markets happen. Recovery is not guaranteed. Recovery *in time* is certainly not guaranteed, because when you need your money, you need it now. But your advisors have let it evaporate.

PART TWO
WHEN THE BEAR EATS YOU

Photo credit: iStock.com/jhorrocks

Why do so many "managed" investors suffer during the various (and inevitable) bear markets? Why do their advisors let the bear gobble up their past gains or profits—and, often a chunk of their original invested capital?

That's what I'll examine with you in these next chapters. I'll be revealing some financial advisory industry practices, beliefs, and strategies (I use that last term very, very loosely) that allow the bear to swallow your money in one gulp.

Understand this: The financial industry is an institution. As such, it's stuck in its ways. It acts as a guild (yes, like in medieval Europe) that lets no one in without vetting them. The industry protects its practices and secrets very closely. It makes sure all guild members toe the line to protect their position.

I needed to write this book so that you would know those secrets and hopefully start gaining the knowledge you need to fight off the bear.

4

THE CURRENT NARRATIVE

Advisory firms want their advisors and all their clients to stay the course. In other words, they don't want their advisors to do much (if anything) to protect your capital. Look at the advice from some of these well-known industry advisors.

Morningstar's "2025 Investment Outlook for Financial Advisors"[27] highlights the value of not overreacting to short-term economic or political events. It stresses the benefits of long-term investing for better outcomes. Yes, the article discusses various international market opportunities. In the end, it still goes with the standard buy-and-hold caution to advisors. But why not react to what the market is currently doing? Why not adjust and adapt? They don't discuss that.

Vanguard's "Advisor's Alpha"[28] framework highlights the value of advisors guiding clients through volatile periods. How, though? By reinforcing long-term investment goals and disciplined (i.e., buy-and-hold) portfolio management.

What kind of management is it when the managers are sitting on their hands?

Merrill Lynch[29] and Ameriprise[30] stress that volatility is a normal part of investing and that—as nervous as it makes their clients seeing the precipitous drop in their portfolio values—the best thing to do is to stay the course. In other words? Do more buy-and-hold. Merrill's chief investment officer (CIO), Kirsten Cabacungan, is quoted as saying, "This market period has been extremely volatile. But when you look at the maximum drawdown so far in the S&P 500, it hasn't breached the 20 percent decline that we typically see in a bear market. After these periods of declines, we historically have seen the index recover—some on average within 10 months." Do you have ten months (and that was just an average, as this CIO revealed) to wait for your portfolio to regain its losses—especially if you're retiring this year? Ameriprise outright advises to just "stand still," let things play out, and "avoid reacting to the news cycle."

If I, Jack Reutemann, say buy-and-hold is not just insane but broken, and then prove it with many other people's data, I'm canceled. I'm banned from the show. I'm blacklisted. If I say, "You don't have to see your portfolio crash and burn—not when your advisor is truly managing your money," I'm shunned by industry big boys. Yet these big brokerage firms get to tell everyone to follow a broken system, lose their shirts, and wait for a return to break even and (maybe) see new gains. I, on the other hand, work to capitalize on market volatility by committing a portion of my clients' funds to participating in both positive and negative short-term trends.

Bear Markets vs. Market Corrections

The current narrative is that if somebody says something institutional is broken—like the stock market—they get blacklisted. That's how messed up our country has become. You can't say something is broken, especially if some power-ful person's or group's big money, political ideology, or power base is behind it.

The simple fact of the matter is that buy-and-hold portfolio management is broken. I don't know how you can call yourself a "money manager" if you let your clients lose 57 percent of their wealth. Insane.

Keep in mind that "official" bear markets are not the only movements to manage for. Those twenty-two official bear markets were -20 percent or greater. If the chart went to -19.95 percent, that wasn't counted, as I've stated. Think about it, though. There's not a whole lot of difference in pain between -19.99 percent and -20.01 percent. Charts and data show another couple of hundred times the S&P 500 has dropped between 10 percent and 19.99 percent. Those aren't called bear markets. Those are euphemistically called "corrections." The talking heads and Pie Chart Promoters (more on them coming up) say, "Oh, we just had a 15 percent correction. What do you mean you lost your job, your wife is divorcing you, and you're going to jump off the building? So sorry."

Listen to Senator Ron Wyden from Oregon testifying before Congress that President Donald Trump has destroyed the stock market, people's retirement accounts, and small businesses.[31] The market's at -18 percent, yes. But solely because of Trump? I don't think so. According to the senator and others like him, it's the end of days. Our wives are going to divorce us. Everybody's going to die.

Stop! The senator and too many others who have viewers and listeners know nothing about investing. Novice investors, beware here. Just because an elected official says it doesn't make it so. This attitude of ignorance and finger-pointing makes me so upset because all those words come out of mouths that have no training, no financial know-how, no verified information.

And above all? They have no solutions.

I have solutions.

Mental/Emotional Distress

Here's the denial. Do you think one word I've written here is on any big broker's website? Can you go to your current financial firm's website and read about a 57 percent loss? No. Do you see them discussing a 34 percent loss? No.

There's no narrative. Even that J.P. Morgan Page 4 Chart is just a bunch of unnarrated statistics. And most of its monthly "Guide to the Markets," by the way, is not understandable to most of its clients. Scroll through it to see how much you understand. Page 4 doesn't have a comment section that says anything even close to "Based on the above chart, maybe you should be careful before you give 100 percent of your money to some unidentified individual at the financial services office in your town." There's no advice, no direction, no management. But it's worse than no management. It's denial of the truth.

I'll tell you what they believe: *We're not going to speak the truth; we're going to deny it even exists. Therefore, people will believe what we tell them and let us buy-and-hold their lifetime savings.*

I think this is the biggest white-collar scam in the history of modern economics.

When you have a bear market, the big firms' so-called experts at money management don't tell people about it on their website. They think, *Close our eyes, shut our mouths, and it won't exist.*

That's the denial piece. To me, that's the glaring omission in their discourse. It would be one thing if they said, "Hey, we want to share some history with you. According to the recorded data . . . blah, blah, blah . . . the S&P 500 has lost more than 20 percent twenty-two times in the last hundred years. Please carefully think through your asset allocation model."

But, here's the out for those buy-and-hold loyalists: Denial is not against the law. It's not illegal, so I guess you can't say it's fraud. But the acts of omission they commit are nonetheless unethical and dishonest. They don't give their clients enough information to make intelligent decisions about their own money, yet they sell themselves as the experts.

I'm sorry that people are dead, divorced, bankrupt, or foreclosed due to losing their wealth in bear markets. It truly breaks my heart because I know the truth. But there comes a tipping point in every circumstance when people want change (or at least answers).

Before I tell you about the tipping point, you need some background. The Financial Industry Regulatory Authority (FINRA) is a private American corporation that regulates itself and member brokerage firms and exchange markets under federal law. I know that's a vague purpose and mission statement, but FINRA is widely known. Today, the US government agency that acts as the ultimate regulator of the US securities industry, including FINRA, is the US Securities and Exchange Commission (SEC),[32] which most people have heard of.

Now, FINRA is a top agency for dealing with complaints. Let's see what FINRA itself said about complaints first in 2008, then in 2009. These statements are straight out of each year's annual report.

"In 2008, FINRA issued 200 formal complaints and 1,007 decisions in formal disciplinary cases. FINRA collected over $28.1 million in fines, either ordered or secured agreements in principle for restitution in excess of $1.0 billion, expelled or suspended 19 firms, barred individuals from the industry and suspended 321 others."[33]

Its 2009 report states, "In 2009, we conducted approximately 2,500 routine examinations and approximately 7,900 cause examinations in response to events such as customer complaints, terminations for cause and regulatory tips."[34]

That's what happened during the 2007–09 bear market.[35] In 2009, there was a spike in customer complaints to FINRA, as you can see by its own statements. Those massive numbers of messages said more or less the same thing: "Plenty of investors lost not only their shirts but their tempers and many could reasonably claim they were deceived by their advisers."[36]

As you see, those are not my words. But as you will also read in these pages, I agree. These advisors were not up to the task of protecting their clients' wealth during the deep decline of that bear market.

Those customer complaints to FINRA, especially in 2008–09, came with the thousands of new mental health visits I told you about. If you think it was just COVID-19 and the quarantining fallout that led massive numbers of people to their shrink, look further into the past. People lost their homes in 2007–09. They lost jobs and wealth in 2007-09. Such a devastating loss! Individuals with money in the markets that had evaporated were now experiencing depression, anxiety, drug and alcohol use, and domestic violence. It led to domestic violence, drunk driving, and other destructive behaviors as people lost their mental and emotional grip. I told you about my seventy-eight-year-old psychologist's booming practice of just this year, 2025. He's old enough in the profession to confirm what I've just said: "It's not the first time."

Lack of money management by so-called money managers was at the root of much of it in 2007–09. I dare say the struggle through the pandemic was almost a piece of cake in comparison.

5
BUY-AND-HOLD
SHOULD BE A CRIME

Of my competitors, 89 percent or more are buy-and-hold "magicians." If you think about magicians and misdirection in general, the whole reason for misdirecting is to distract the public from a painful reality.

The painful reality is that your advisor is stuck in a wealth-killing buy-and-hold standstill. Your advisor charges you a fee for managing your money but isn't managing your money.

The Buy-and-Hold Narrative

Before you protest, that 89 percent of advisors I've been referencing is not just a number I made up. See this Smart-Asset article from November 8, 2022: "Despite recent stock market shocks, most clients and advisors are either *staying the course or buying the dip*. About *89% of advisors* say that their clients are employing one of those two strategies. The figure is even higher for the percentage of advisors recommending either action, at *close to 94%*" (emphasis mine).[37]

Doesn't this mean 89–94 percent of advisors are doing buy-and-hold or buying the dip?

Later in the article, we read, "Bear markets are a natural part of an investment cycle," said Ryan Barber from VantagePointe Financial in Saginaw, Michigan. "*Stay the course*. Better yet, buy the dip" (emphasis mine).

It's followed by this comment: "Beyond understanding the bear market as part of a larger investment cycle, many advisors recommend looking at your portfolio over the long-term."

All of those comments ("stay the course," "looking at your portfolio over the long-term," etc.) are just stealthy, sneaky ways of saying those advisors are doing buy-and-hold.

In other words? They would hold. They wouldn't do a thing. They would make no changes to their clients' holdings to protect their wealth. *They admitted they wouldn't lift a finger to protect your money.* That's insane!

This means at least 89 percent of advisors use a buy-and-hold strategy that doesn't protect investors.

There are about 300,000 licensed investment advisors. A chunk of them are staff (if you have staff speaking to a client and doing paperwork, they still have to have a license). That leaves around 100,000 investment advisors actually working with clients.

This 89 percent response was an absolutely embarrassing, shocking answer to me. The whole industry should've been red-faced. But no. These were professional respondents, not random people in the streets. These were licensed investment advisors.

- Less than 11 percent said, "I would take defensive action, meaning I'm going to sell. I'm going short. I'm going to move to bonds. I'm going to stocks that are thriving. I'm going to do *something*."
- Fully 89–94 percent of the respondents said, "We would continue to buy and hold our portfolio."

One of the biggest lies in my industry is "The market always comes back." It does eventually. That's technically true. But it might take thirteen years.

If you go to the Page 4 Chart, you'll see the stock market high in February 2000. It then crashed. It didn't get back to those levels until May 2013. It took thirteen years and three months for the S&P 500 to break even—to get back to where it was in March 2000.

You just know that some knucklehead at some big brokerage firm is going to say, "See? See, there's proof that buy-and-hold works. It always comes back. Oh well, so it took thirteen years. But it came back, didn't it?"

Sure. But how many people died of old age, committed suicide, or walked away from the card game during those thirteen years? How many didn't have thirteen years to wait for their money?

I've been doing technical analysis and stock market charting since 1987. Based on that survey plus other things I've read, my firm, unshakable, unwavering belief is this:

If you're going to pay somebody a management fee, you should get some management.

The reason it's called a management fee is you're supposed to receive management. Buy-and-hold, in my book, is not "passive" management. It's zero management.

By the way, do you remember my earlier tables of market losses and time to recover? The SEC and FINRA collect massive fees from firms across the financial sector. Together, they've institutionalized the buy-and-hold narrative—and prolonged the time to recover, I believe.

Some advisors protest that buy-and-hold is just *one* of their strategies. They say management strategies have evolved over time. They say the buy-and-hold strategy is "valid right now." Boy, do I get angry when I hear that.

The evolution is real, sure. Let me run a timeline by you that my team recently collated. You'll see the rise of buy-and-hold among CFP® and other finance industry professionals. You'll see a shift in advisor mindset over time.

Timeline of Investment Advisor Philosophies

1950s–70s: Rise of Modern Portfolio Theory

- Harry Markowitz (1952) introduced modern portfolio theory (MPT) and the focus shifted to diversification and more risk-adjusted returns.
- Buy-and-hold started to take root, but only in a sort of academic way, and most brokers still followed stock-picking and sales-based models. The latter was common because investment advisors were still rare; brokers dominated, earning commissions on trades and products.

1980s: Development of Financial Planning

- The Certified Financial Planner (CFP®) designation, established in 1972, began gaining momentum in the 1980s.
- John Bogle founded Vanguard (1975). He championed index fund investing, a major buy-and-hold milestone.
- Brokers still dominated. Early fee-based advisors began using strategic asset allocation and long-term planning.
- Personal computing was on the rise. It was the early days of software development for PCs.

1990s: Advent of Asset Allocation and Passive Investing
- Academic research showed that asset allocation (distributing investments across different asset classes like stocks, bonds, and cash) explains over 90 percent of portfolio returns. Profitable investing was not about stock selection alone.
- Mutual funds and index funds proliferated. Advisors began adopting diversified model portfolios.
- The RIA (registered investment advisor) model[38] began gaining popularity, and advisors charged AUM (assets under management) fees. More and more, they used buy-and-hold ETF (exchange-traded fund) and mutual fund strategies.

2000s: The Dot-Com Bubble Burst and the Rise of Fee-Based Advice
- The dot-com crash (2000–02) and the financial crisis (2007–09) pushed investors toward risk-managed, long-term approaches.
- Buy-and-hold gained credibility as market timing proved unreliable.
- Advisors shifted more heavily into strategic asset allocation, emphasizing financial planning over stock-picking.
- Dimensional Fund Advisors (DFAs) and Vanguard firms expanded dramatically among advisors.

- Technical analysis software and algorithmic trading were on the rise.

2010s: Buy-and-Hold Becomes the Norm
- Passive strategies dominated and ETF usage exploded. Robo-advisors emerged; these were digital platforms providing automated, algorithm-driven financial planning and investment services with little to no human supervision.
- Companies such as Wealthfront and Betterment began promoting automated buy-and-hold portfolios.
- Fiduciary standard gained momentum (yet by 2022, most advisors were still not fiduciaries), requiring any advisor who held a CFP® designation to be a fiduciary. Earning this designation required years of coursework and experience, passing a challenging exam, and adherence to the CFP® Board's Code of Ethics and Standards of Conduct.[39]
- Most with RIA and CFP® designations adopted long-term, low-cost, diversified portfolios using buy-and-hold as the foundation. Tactical/active management strategies still existed but mainly in niche or high-net-worth segments.

2020s: Buy-and-Hold Dominates

- Analysts attribute market volatility to the COVID-19 fallout, inflation, and a burgeoning AI-driven tech boom. This sparks interest in tactical overlays. Core strategies remain buy-and-hold.
- Advisors use behavioral coaching with clients, mostly to retain them in the buy-and-hold model, even and especially when the client is panicking. They offer financial planning and tax optimization, not stock-picking, as their value proposition.
- Model portfolios and outsourced chief investment officer (CIO) services are on the rise. This makes buy-and-hold even easier for small firms.

Just like any institution in this country, the financial industry has seen layers upon layers added to it. If I dare say it's partially or completely broken, though, the institutional folks don't like it.

6
BUY-AND-HOLD PIE
CHART PROMOTERS

Here's the process those passive "managers" use on you:
A new client takes a test (with pretty stupid questions).
Based on the test results and your age—no matter what
your answers are—you get put into a 60/40 model, which
is typically 60 percent growth, 40 percent income/indexed. I
call that "the S&P 500 pie chart."

First, when they stick you in the S&P 500 pie chart,
you're not getting money management. You're now stuck in
their buy-and-hold institution. You have non-management.
Those advisors aren't portfolio managers. They're relationship managers. That's not what you need to protect and grow
your wealth in a manner that is, if not wholly predictable, at
least data-driven and honest.

Second, that 60/40 pie chart doesn't represent your
personal risk tolerance—which is why you thought you were

taking that test. The pie chart is cookie-cutter-style investing. It assumes your needs and investing expectations are the same as everyone else's. It's a terrible assumption to make, but it's the easiest one for the large investment houses.

You can always find one of the infamous pie charts when you thumb through your company's 401(k) provider website. The pie chart shows you how your company retirement plan account is currently invested in a mixture of stocks, bonds, and money market funds. Easy to understand and visualize.

Most financial advisors would be willing to show you how your investable funds should be invested now, in pie chart living color. This core investment management advice concept hasn't changed in over seventy-five years.

Many investors think the pie chart protects them from market declines. They end up surprised. Merely being invested in different types of stocks and bonds isn't good enough anymore. It's not enough protection from the bear—not by far. I'll talk more about this in a coming chapter.

For now, here's the big picture of pie chart investing. It isn't pretty.

- The asset allocations in a pie chart don't work very well when the stock market is going down.
- Pie charts are static, unable to turn on a dime or adjust to constantly changing worldwide political, economic, and stock market events. They can't react to budget deficits, bank failures,

recessions, real estate price depressions, record unemployment levels, CEO scandals, or foreign governments defaulting on their debt.
- They have no memory of market history. They ignore the fact of past bear markets and negative returns of the S&P 500.
- Pie charts are based on the assumption that stock market investment returns will always be positive.
- They can't predict your future investment returns.
- They can't help you define or manage your investment risk level.

You don't want an advisor to stick you in a pie chart. That means they "set it and forget it" until you complain about losing 34 percent in a bear market they didn't protect you from.

Humans, not preset pie charts, have to make investment management decisions in reaction to those events as they happen.

The Pie Chart and True Diversification

Do more slices imply greater diversity? Unfortunately, even though a pie chart can make it look like an investor is safely diversified, it's probably not the case. For many investors, the pie chart can be misleading. It's sold to you as a protective mechanism. You're led to believe the allocations in your portfolio mean one portion rises in a bull market, and one portion protects you in a bear market.

No, no, no. Diversification isn't protection, though managers like you to believe so. Investors are probably much less protected than they realize. Well, you realize it when the bear comes running in and gobbles up your wealth. But by then it's too late.

Do Mutual Funds Diversify Your Investment?

Here's something that makes matters worse. Investors with multiple mutual funds often own the exact same companies across the different funds. We call this phenomenon "stock overlap" or "stock intersection." You may own ten different mutual funds, but the largest holdings in each fund are the exact same companies. It's amazing to me how many investors don't know this. And it's appalling to me that advisors do this to their clients. If you love Apple so much, just buy Apple stock all on its own.

Yet advisors call this a diversification of your portfolio. Don't believe it.

A fascinating study in the late 1970s by Elton and Gruber[40] concluded that a portfolio's diversity stopped improving once it had more than thirty different securities. In other words, increasing from one or two securities up to thirty led to a big improvement, but increasing from thirty to a thousand different securities didn't.

Most mutual funds (and this is wildly variable, so excuse me for the range) hold between fifty and two hundred different stocks. That's far more than Elton and Gruber's maximum of thirty.

Consider that the next time you open up your quarterly statement. How many mutual funds do you own? How many individual stocks are inside all those mutual funds? What's the overlap?

The Bear and Real Fee-Based Management

Brokerage firm brokers, such as Morgan Stanley, Merrill Lynch, Wells Fargo Advisors, and UBS, are not real fee-based investment advisors.[41] Most brokerage firm employees are W-2 staff with a contract and therefore can't be independent advisors with custodians.

Here's why I mention this: These advisors have no sell-side discipline. First, this means they rarely issue "sell" recommendations on their biggest clients' stocks. They're devoted to the buy-and-hold Kool-Aid. Second, their stock salesmen are all expected to sell stocks or funds that their company has underwritten.

Remember when I said the financial industry acts like a medieval guild? This is more proof.

Bear markets are going to happen: They've happened twenty-two times in the last ninety-nine years, not to mention over a hundred declines of less than 20 percent.

When it happens again, what is the guild's plan to protect your assets from an average 38 percent fall? There is no plan, as 89 percent of advisors have admitted. Buy-and-hold. Wait for the market to rise again.

7
PORTFOLIO MANAGEMENT? I THINK NOT!

Money management is what is done for you with money you have saved and wish to invest. You expect the manager to invest, protect, and grow your money, of course.

Clients imagine their manager uses technical analysis software. They imagine their manager has loads of resources available to do this work.

It's true: We do.

Every finance professional can access, use, and understand the software. A team of people in my office spends six or eight hours a day using the technical, analytical software. This is daily work in my firm. The team is looking at all the markets and thousands of stocks every day. This is not something clients paying for such a service should have to learn. It's part of our "money management" work.

As far as getting into and understanding the high value of technical analysis goes, I got very, very lucky.

Analysis and Money Management

I can't say I planned it. I was at a big convention in 1997. I went to a breakout session. A guy named Tom Dorsey was speaking, and I thought, *Wow, this guy knows what the hell he's talking about.* At that time, the man was very famous, and he's still considered one of the pioneers in technical analysis.[42]

He wrote a well-known book, *Point and Figure Charting: The Essential Application for Forecasting and Tracking Market Prices*, in 1987. But, today we don't have to do this charting and analysis with a pencil and grid paper like he did. When he wrote the book in 1987, no internet or software to speak of existed, of course.

Today at my firm, we use an extremely sophisticated charting software called TC2000®. It's the gold standard now, a super-serious software for technical market analysis.

Let me take you back to our J.P. Morgan Page 4 Chart.

As you look at those bear markets, what are you concerned about? You might be worried about safety in your community, Putin's next moves, the rising cost of living for your kids, war in the Middle East, the kind of education your grandkids should get so they can make it in life—and how they can pay for those educations. You might be distressed about the kind of world we've set up for them to inhabit. When you start to worry, it snowballs.

I know it and hear it when a new client comes into my firm. When we're interviewing each other, I ask, "Who are your current advisors?"

They say, "I'm with some idiot at _____ (Please . . . fill in the blank for yourself) who never calls me."

I always propose, "Let me tell you a little bit about our firm."

The first thing I do is I pull out the Page 4 Chart. Go look at it like that prospective client of ours would: What are you worried about? When do you plan to retire? How sure are you that your money will be there for you—without waiting for a bounce-back after a dramatic bear market?

No Management from Managers

I'll say this a lot, so get used to it: When they stick you in a pie chart, that's not money management. You shouldn't have to pay a management fee for someone to put you in an investment that you could've made all on your own in your self-directed online account.

When you pay for management, look them in the eye and ask, "So how are you going to manage my money? I'm not into this whole buy-and-hold thing." And expect an answer. As you keep reading, I'll give you more understanding and more ammunition to demand that your advisor explain how they're providing management.

When you invest your money with any financial advisory firm, you believe you're hiring a professional to actively track, manage, and protect your wealth. You're right to expect just that. You don't expect them to ignore the risks due to a bear market that's brewing.

I did promise not to get deep into the weeds of technical analysis with you in this book. But let me nonetheless give you a taste of what it looks like for my team and me every day as we protect your wealth from the bears. *We* don't ignore it. We know that bear markets come every 4.7 years on average. We know that our job is to both protect and grow your money. One way we do that is with stock charts. What is an easy way to read charts? Use the color-coded candlestick charts that I use, like figure 3.[43]

Figure 3. Understanding Candlestick Charts

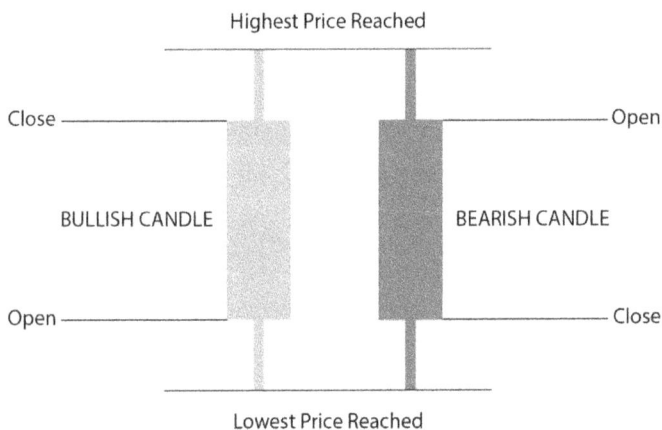

On a candlestick chart (and you see a number of them in this book), any red rectangle is a declining day for prices, while any green rectangle is a rising price day. The height of the rectangle shows the open price to the close price for the day. If there's a wick up, that means there was an intraday high (the day's highest price). If there's a wick down, that means there was an intraday low (the day's lowest price).

In my firm's charting software (TC2000®),[44] I click directly under the candlestick to see that the closing price was, say, $585. I might also see that the high was, say, $598. The wicks show me the day's highest and lowest prices. No lower wick? It means the lowest price that day was also the opening price. Use the same rule for the missing upper wick.

Side note: Did you know that McGraw-Hill (the textbook publishing company) acquired Standard & Poor's? Not the index. They bought the financial services company that created and manages the S&P 500 index. This acquisition took place in 1966. They've got all these academics that slice and dice.

Now, where am I going with this? I don't mean to be an egomaniac, but 99 percent of the public doesn't have a clue about charting. Investing novices don't know about this yet. Many people have never heard of candlestick charts and don't realize the stock market is anywhere near this complex. Most of the time, they don't even want to learn about it. (A little later in the book, I'll explain it in a way that's easy to understand.)

For me, that's fine. Technical analysis is a professional skill that takes training. My team and I have that skill, and it's part of what we provide as portfolio management to our clients. They come to us so they don't have to learn and do this themselves, after all.

The Big Fraud

But then I think about the 89 percent-plus of professional investment advisors. They also don't understand anything I just said. And I get angry again. The big fraud? That 89 percent calls themselves investment *advisors*. Their clients believe they get skilled, educated, and active management of their money from these "advisors."

They don't. Financial advisors are, in fact, only relationship managers. They bring in assets to be managed, then turn around and give your money to the staff in the basement of their home office. That staff creates a pie chart. Many of them are not even good at the relationship thing, if clients who leave them and come to us at RFS are any indication. "I never hear from my advisor!" is a common complaint that pisses me off.

I have a friend who used to do Human Resources for a big Washington, DC, bank called Chevy Chase Bank and Trust. Chevy Chase Bank was merged into Capital One and officially became inactive on July 30, 2009,[45] so I feel I can tell you this story.

You're not going to believe this. My friend said to me, "I only hire extremely good-looking women and extremely handsome men to sit in the lobby. Their whole job is to greet and direct clients coming in. When the older man with money walks in, he's going to go to the hot twenty-five-year-old female greeter. And when the older woman with half a million dollars comes in, she's going to go to the buff, handsome twenty-five-year-old male greeter. They're our magnets."

Even knowing this industry, I was sort of gobsmacked at the blatant admission. "Are you making this up?" Yes, I'd heard this myth, this urban legend, but really?

He insisted he wasn't. "No. Stop into one of my lobbies one day. I don't hire old, ugly people. I hire the best-looking, youngest people I can find to sit in my lobby. I don't give a flying hoot what they know or don't know about investing. Those beautiful people only need to draw in prospective clients. That's all. Then our guys come out of the back offices to build a relationship. It starts with a pretty or handsome face that's drawn them into the bank and invited them to sit a minute."

That was the Human Resources manager at Chevy Chase Bank and Trust in Chevy Chase, Maryland. Every time I've walked into a bank since then, I've seen that he's right. Every bank. There might be some older staff behind the teller cages, but there are no old, ugly people sitting in the lobby.

Let's be clear. I have no direct knowledge of what went on at that bank back then. This story came to me from the man who used this particular hiring strategy. But since I've spent my career in this industry, I can attest to the fact that the "pretty people" story has floated around for a long time. It's never been a rule or a formal requirement to hold any banking job. But the stories have swung from myth to trend to reality more often than most people realize.[46]

It's just that being attractive probably helps, as this HR professional said, especially in roles that involve direct client interaction such as what occurs in a bank's lobby or reception service.[47] Attractiveness, going beyond the physical and into effective management and effective interpersonal skills (a.k.a. flattery, in my mind),[48] is also taught in our industry. I've said it before: Most financial advisors are relationship managers first and foremost.

Most of the people I listen to on Fox News, I think, are pretty intelligent. But it's amazing that (except Greg Gutfeld) every single person you see on Fox News is also young and pretty (just kidding, Greg—I think you're great).

8
THE BIGGEST
WHITE-COLLAR SCAM

Your question by now is surely, "How do I protect myself from the Pie Chart Promoters? How do I know that my money manager is *managing*? How do I know they're protecting my money (when needed) and growing my money (as much as possible) for me?"

Those Red Flags

A very newly minted attorney came to me from a wealthy family. We were interviewing each other. She was in her twenties and was just starting to earn her living but had some bequeathed money to manage too. Her dad had referred her to his advisor at one of those brokerage firms I really hate to name (and for once will not), who was glad to take on this new client. She exploded when she realized the advisor had put her in the same 20/80 pie chart as her near-retirement father. This was even after she had filled out the so-called risk tolerance questionnaire.

Now, let me remind you of your pie chart lesson. Only 20 percent of her money was in growth investments, and 80 percent was in very conservative, low-to-no-growth investments—at age twenty. She had at least forty years of practice as (presumably) a highly paid attorney to save, invest, and generate wealth.

She got it. It was smart of her to explode. Even smarter, though, was moving her money. After some interviewing here and there, she brought it to us. I was thrilled that she refused pie charts. She was thrilled that I'd never put her in one.

First, remember that when any financial advisor puts you into *any* pie chart, they haven't paid attention to your wishes and goals or your stated risk tolerance. That's my educated guess, knowing how these nitwits operate. It's a red flag waving in your face. That young attorney saw the flag, and now you should be able to as well.

Does that pie chart financial advisor ignore your anxiety? Do they pretend you're not wringing your hands? Sure. They tell you, "Oh, yes, we see the market is moving somewhat downward. Be patient. It will bounce back. Hold on. Don't sell. Don't move out of your current positions. It always rises again."

That's not management.

Denying that a bear market will wipe out your wealth is what they do. It's a red flag telling you that you're with the wrong advisors. Like the young attorney, you would be right to explode and then move your money. Money is not stationary. It moves. Move it.

Not asking you about your wishes for your money management is what they do. Not respecting your comments about your risk tolerance or lack thereof is also what they do. They don't care what your responses to that risk tolerance questionnaire were. You're stuck in their pie chart. You're stuck in their firm's in-house investment products, including mutual funds that don't beat the S&P 500 (and perhaps never have, not one year). You're stuck paying those fees.

They ignore questions like, "How could my money do better than it's doing now?" You're in a buy-and-hold nightmare. The red flags are waving.

Go to your Pie Chart Promoter's website, and you might read something right on their home page along the lines of, "We're bullish. We encourage all our advisors to stay the course."

If you read *that* when the S&P 500 is already down, sitting at -18 percent and showing no signs of rising, that's a red flag. It says you're in that buy-and-hold grip. It announces that the bear is going to eat you alive (and probably already is).

When the bear has eaten 34 percent of your wealth during that devastating fall in the markets, those Pie Chart Promoters have no words of comfort for you. They repeat their mantra: "Hold on. It always bounces back." They certainly have no explanation for how they let your wealth evaporate in that bear market in the first place.

Last but not least, if an advisor is not transparent about their fees, run.[49] You need the truth, the whole truth, and nothing but the truth here. That naturally includes revealing all fees they're legally obliged to disclose. But it also includes the ones they're not. See that red flag and start running.

Big, bright, waving red flags. They should make you hustle yourself right out the door and away from that advisor right now.

What they have done to your wealth is not illegal. It's not against the law to put your money in lackluster investments. But it makes me angry. They're not acting as fiduciaries, who by definition must act in your best interests, not theirs.

They are not financial advisors or money managers. They're charging you a fee to do nothing.

9
WHY I HAD TO WRITE THIS BOOK

I guess by now you can pretty well guess why I had to write this book.

I've seen enough. Learned a lot. Understood how those big boys of finance maneuver. I've seen the human fallout of mental health collapses and worse when clients (not mine, and thank you to all my teachers in the industry) have suffered sequence-of-returns disasters right at retirement.

When I started out in the world of work, I didn't have a financial career in mind.

I was a young man when I answered an ad about door-to-door sales to make money, so I went to the interview. The sales pitch was that you go to all the local high schools and talk to the principals or whoever is in charge. You identify the girls who aren't going to college but who are getting jobs. (Really. I'm not kidding. Welcome back to the 1970s.)

You have a prospectus book and a demo set. You make them a lunch or dinner with your set of cookware. You sell the cookware and add-ons of tableware like china and crystal stemware to single working girls who aren't going to college.

After the interview, I explained all this to my father and mother in one breath.

They said, "A direct sales job? You've lost your mind!"

I said, "Well, I'm going to try it."

I dove in full steam ahead (my usual speed, in other words), and at the end of that first year, I came in number eleven in the country out of three thousand salespeople.

The next year they made me a manager, which put fifteen salespeople under me. I came in fourth in the country that year. The next year, they made me manager of all of Baltimore and Washington, DC, with six groups of fifteen kids under me. I came in number two in the country that third year. And, of course, I earned money.

I submitted this info to the local career placement center to see if I could get a better position. It was 1972, and there was no Google or Amazon for job searching. I put all this down on paper: "Reutemann number eleven, Reutemann number four, Reutemann number two." The placement center did the job, and my phone started ringing off the hook. I got calls from recruiters at IBM, General Motors, Ford, Xerox, Kodak, and Polaroid.

Wow! At that age, it sure looked like everybody on earth wanted to hire me. All my friends were saying, "Reutemann, you know your grades are okay, but you're not a 4.0. You'll fall flat on your ugly face if you take one of those jobs."

I just said, "Dude, they're not calling me because of a 4.0 grade average. It's because I can sell!"

It was the IBM recruiters who said, "You have more sales skills than a thirty-year-old who's been selling our typewriters for ten years."

Anyway, I ended up going with a well-known company in Minneapolis, Minnesota. Investors Diversified Services was acquired by American Express in 1984. At the time, they were IDS and had their name on the tallest tower in town.

In November 1972, I got my Maryland state life/annuity and health license. I got my certification as a financial professional (CFP®) in 1978 and kept it active for these many uninterrupted years. My license number is four digits—today there are hundreds of thousands with the certification, so I was on board in the earliest days.

I've been a CFP® for all these years. It's a commonly known fact in our industry that those of us with the certification take care of only the 6 percent richest population. That means 94 percent of people either don't have access to a CFP® or would know to go to one but can't afford it.

On top of that, many brokerage firms don't take on new clients who have less than $500,000 to invest. Sometimes they set the bar even higher. They position themselves as "high-net-worth advisors." It cuts out a lot of people for whom I'm writing this book (and I hope you investing novices are still reading).

I know this huge 94 percent audience is suffering from a combination of no information and misinformation. I know there's a conspiracy among the big banks and brokerage firms to avoid the truth in their advertising. And no one's calling them on it—except me.

I started my firm in June 1975. Do the math—I've been in the business for fifty years. What we have today is the RIA (registered investment advisor), which is 99 percent at Schwab, with a bit at Fidelity. Schwab has always been good to me. Never lied. Never tried to hoodwink us. A good firm.

The Origin of This Book Is a Gorilla

As I've said, I've been doing technical analysis since 1987, and I put some really outstanding numbers on the board. Disclaimer: When I say, "on the board," I mean for all my clients but also for myself and my employees. Success leaves a trace.

This is based on feedback from new clients and from disgruntled advisors with CFP designations in other firms. Advisors tell their clients how they will be managing their money. They say nothing about how they'll protect it. They have no comment on how to grow it except buy-and-hold.

At my office, we take advantage of technical analysis. We don't do that thing that Warren Buffett is so famous for warning against: We don't do emotional buying and selling. We don't sell because everyone's afraid. We don't buy because everyone is greedy. We look at the data. We look at the technical indicators. Yes, it's emotionless decision-making for us. It's still an exciting way to protect our clients' wealth and grow it for them.

We listen to our clients' statements about their risk tolerance or lack thereof. We don't make risk management decisions based on emotions or some talking head's commentary. Our decision-making—whether it's to trade in or out, or to actually do some of that buy-and-hold—is all based on "quantitative momentum." In other words, we use measurable, rules-based criteria.

My success for clients is closely related not only to learning and fully understanding our analytical tools but also to using the results of our team's technical market analysis. In all my years in this profession, I've come to know for a fact that all financial professionals have access to technical analysis. I also see that they don't use it.

During the Great Recession of October 2007 to March 2009, the S&P 500 lost 57 percent of its value. It was catastrophic for investors to lose that much, and I think everyone gets that.

There's a gentleman named Bill Good who's internationally famous. He started a marketing, sales, and operations company called Bill Good Gorilla Marketing in 1988–89. He claims he invented the first CRM (customer relationship management) software. No one has ever contradicted him, including Salesforce, which is the recognized leader today and has actually adopted CRM as its stock symbol. The mid-to-late eighties were the very, very early days of software applications and computing in general. It was all just becoming available, not only to smaller businesses but to mainstream consumers.

Anyway, what Bill created was a CRM for investment advisors. He called it (you guessed it) Gorilla and sold it to 60,000–70,000 people in its earliest days. Of course, my firm bought, trained on, and started using Gorilla very early too. It was the most complete tool he could make for financial advisors, and it's still great. It's in its fifth iteration today. In addition to being a CRM, it has a library of content with thousands of seminars, letters, and prospecting campaigns. You name it, it's there.

Bill had "laws" for developing relationships with clients. One is that you have to contact your clients two hundred times a year. His software already allowed users to record every one of those touches. He practices all this himself, as you'll see.

Side note: Go look at the Page 4 Chart to refresh your memory. You'll see that when Bill Good called me up in January 2009, the bear wasn't done eating us alive. The Page 4 Chart will remind you that inside the Great Recession of -57 percent from October 2007 to March 2009 was calendar year 2008, when the S&P 500 was at -38 percent, which became part of the -57 percent. I told you that when the S&P 500 was measuring -57 percent in a bear market, RFS was at only -4 percent for its clients.

With that in mind, fast-forward. In the 2007–09 bear market, Bill had access to thousands of advisors who were his clients. I knew he was reaching out for a reason. He always kept his finger on the pulse of the industry. He asked how I was doing, how the firm was doing, and how we were doing for our clients.

I said, "We're doing great. We had our best year in the history of the company. We added about $45 million of new assets."

Bill was a little surprised (but pleased, at least from his voice). "Jack, the S&P 500 was -38 percent last year."

I said, "Bill, we had the best year in the history of the company. We added $45 million of new assets and, of course, many new clients. Sorry, but I'd have to go look up how many. And just so you know? We are not, I repeat *not*, at -38 percent here at RFS."

Bill was excited now. "Jack, every single advisor I'm talking to is in hiding. They're afraid. They're afraid to go to the grocery store. They're afraid to go to church. Let me get back to you."

Bill called me back about three weeks later. "Jack, I've been calling all my top gorillas, and I found one person who did exactly what you did."

"Oh, who's that?"

"His name is Rick Lager from Minneapolis."

I laughed and laughed, not surprised. "Bill, I've known Rick Lager for a long time. I was in Tom Dorsey's training way back when with Rick Lager. We text and email each other on a regular basis." Tom Dorsey, of Dorsey Wright and Associates, is the grandfather of technical analysis.

Then came some of the greatest, most profound words
to ever come out of Bill Good's mouth: "I smell a seminar."

He said, "My team and I are going to do an invitation.
We're outlining everything you and Rick did during this
market for your clients and how the two of you were -1
percent when everybody else was -38 percent. We're going
to do a seminar, and you guys are going to create and present the content, and we're going to charge Gorilla advisors
$2,500 for four days with you both. It's going to start on
Thursday at three and end on Sunday at four, and you need
to come up with a name."

I smell a seminar. Yes, indeed! Rick and I put our heads
together. Coming up with twenty hours of content was
like asking me to take a shower. And we came up with a
name . . .

The No More Pies Seminar

We came up with what we still think is a clever name. We
called it No More Pies. And people asked us, "Is this like a
cooking class? Is this about a diet?"

Now, you've read this far with me, so you have a
better guess than that about where Rick and I were going
with the name.

We told everyone, "It refers to pie charts created by
those buy-and-hold morons who lost 57 percent of your
money during the Great Recession. The name of the class is
No More Pies, and it's about getting away from pie charts.
We're going to teach you how Rick and I were at -4 percent

when you were at -57 percent. Do you think that might be worthwhile for you and your clients? Is that something you would like to know?"

We did the first No More Pies class in June 2009, when we had about ninety people in Bill Good's conference rooms in Salt Lake City. We continued to do one every ninety days. We crisscrossed the country. San Diego to Boston. Seattle to Miami. We did forty-seven No More Pies seminars before COVID-19, the last in January 2020. Since then we've been doing them informally on the internet. Approximately 2,400 people went through the class, and it was a huge success.

Eighty-Sixed from CNBC

Some chapters ago, I hinted that I had been canceled from presenting on TV. It's true. It was my late press agent who got me out on a financial TV news circuit by telling them, "You want to talk to the guy who was -4 percent when everybody was -57 percent." In other words, my success spoke volumes. My agent got me on various financial news shows at major televised financial broadcast programs seventy-two times.

Then, in July 2012, my press agent called me and said, "I've got some really bad news, Jack. The networks informed me that you're no longer welcome on TV . . . ever again."

I wanted to know the reason.

She said (and I'm paraphrasing), "You've pissed off their advertisers. They're sick and tired of hearing you trashing buy-and-hold and bashing pie charts. They're sick of how you insult them because their clients are paying a fee for being -57 percent. Basically, they've all told the networks it's time to choose either them and their advertising money or you. So you're no longer allowed on those networks."

Now, everything went through my agent, which is the point of having an agent. So I didn't hear exactly who told her all this, but I trusted her. I also won't tell you who the advertisers might be on financial news shows, though you can deduce by now that I really want to name them. You can speculate on your own.

We've all heard about newscasters and TV presenters getting eighty-sixed for low viewership and low ratings. Advertisers are the news channels' money source, and they have a say about who, how, and what those networks promote as well.

You would have thought this was the McCarthy[50] hearings in the mid-twentieth century, when US Senator Joseph McCarthy said, "You are a communist! You are on the blacklist! You are shunned! You are canceled. You are out of luck and out of work!"

I am no longer welcome on financial newscasts or programs. Why? I'm telling viewers the truth. Like McCarthy often blacklisted Americans without proof, so do big networks. If the networks don't or won't do proper research, it's the viewers who are not properly informed.

Then a financial network goes and retains talking heads like Jim Cramer. This boggles my mind. According to Wikipedia (as of August 28, 2025), "Jim Cramer is an American television personality, author, entertainer, and former hedge fund manager." Best known as the host of CNBC's *Mad Money*, he's one of the most visible financial commentators in the United States. It's unfortunate, in my mind, that people see him as a "financial guru" while his official profile first calls him a "TV personality." The latter is more to the point as far as I'm concerned.

Yes, he's popular as a "stock picker." But analyses of his written calls have found his accuracy rate for buys is only around 47 percent.[51] That's slightly lower than random chance. It's lower than the rates of some other market strategists. And his sell recommendations come in at around 42 percent accuracy. Cramer's reputation for being wrong has become a running joke in financial circles.[52] People find it so funny that a sort of counterculture has emerged from his messes. It has investors overtly betting against his positions. (And I'm the one who gets eighty-sixed?)

Cramer is energetic, I'll give him that—but his zany theatrical style seems to prioritize entertainment over reliable financial advice.[53] In contrast to me, his advertisers have always loved him. They must, or he wouldn't be an institution on the network.

Novice investors, beware who you believe. Beware of all the talking heads on financial networks. Ask yourself, "Is this talking head only an entertainer or a skilled analyst?" Then do more research.

Yes, I'm still appalled when I think about being disinvited from the financial network programs. I'm a very successful businessman, and I'm disgusted at how people—Americans who've worked hard for their money and put their trust in someone calling themselves a professional money manager—are being treated.

So now you know why I had to write this book.

10
A LITTLE MATH TO SCARE YOU

Now, I have to come clean. I've said that advisors put you in a 60/40 pie chart. While that's largely true (60/40 is the most commonly used "formula"), it's not the whole story about pie charts.

The Pie Chart Portfolio Explained

Most investment advisors have seven investment models or pie chart options. There might be organizations that have more or fewer than that.

The growth pie chart is called 100/0. The first number refers to concentration in stocks, a.k.a. "growth." If you're 100/0, you're in for 100 percent growth; you have zero fixed-income investments.

Then there's the fixed-income model, which is 0/100, meaning you have no stocks and are positioned for zero growth; you are 100 percent fixed-income.

And then between the two, we have those ninety-eight shades of gray. In theory, there are a hundred investment models.

But usually, in addition to the two bookends of 100/0 and 0/100, the majority of firms just offer 80/20, 60/40, 40/60, and 20/80, for a total of six models.

You'll recall my young attorney client whose advisor (shared with her father) committed the insanity of putting her in the same 20/80 pie chart they put her father in. These models exist. That doesn't mean they're the right pie.

On top of that, there are two delivery systems. If you have enough money, you meet with a live person at a big firm like Morgan Stanley. Or you work with a fee-based registered investment advisor (RIA) like Schwab. You look the advisor in the eyes. You have a dialogue. That's one delivery system.

The other delivery system is to dial the 800 number at, say, Vanguard (this process is pretty universal). You get twenty-five-year-old non-advisors on the phone. They ask you some questions, mostly to get your email address. They email you the questionnaire, such as the Vanguard Asset Allocation Investment Questionnaire. You fill it out, do the DocuSign thing, and send it back.

When the twenty-five-year-old non-advisor calls you back, he announces, "Mrs. Jefferson, you tested 60/40." Like you won the lottery.

He goes on. "That's 60 percent growth, 40 percent fixed-income." As if you'll understand. He doesn't explain.

He has no idea whether you know what he's talking about. He never utters the words "risk tolerance."

"I believe you told me you were fifty-five years old and in pretty good health, so I'm okay with 60/40," he says.

He's okay with it? What?! Wait! No, no, no! What the—?

He's still talking. "But I want you to know what that means. Your money is going to be 60 percent concentrated in stock-type funds for growth and 40 percent concentrated in fixed-income funds. Are you okay with that?"

Aw, no, *please!*

So first, you're not dealing with a financial advisor at all. The 800 number guy has no idea who you are. At this point, you haven't sat with an advisor. You've been able to ask zero questions.

And second? Just no. I would definitely not be "okay with that."

Let's say you, reading this book, are fifty-five years old. You now know more than the guy on the 800 line. You know that at least one bear market (and how about those future ones you'll be staring at?) took *thirteen years* just to break even. You also know this: You're retiring at age sixty, which the 800 hotline kid probably never asked you. You definitely, unmistakably, and clearly expressed a *very low* tolerance to risk in the questionnaire.

The non-financial person on the phone seemed to ignore all this. And you were going to be expected to give up your life savings to a stranger putting you in a 60/40?

No. I'm not okay with any of that. You shouldn't be okay with it, either.

Sequence-of-Returns Risk: The Real Math

I've presented to you a phenomenon called the sequence-of-returns risk. Let's see how that risk applies to the 60/40 blend during a bear market.

First, a reminder. Most Pie Chart Promoters want you to trust and believe that the 40 percent of your money in the "fixed-income funds" is protected during a bear market.

By now, I'd like to trust and believe your skepticism is rising to the surface.

Say you're 100 percent in the stock market with a $2 million portfolio value at the peak just before this bear market. Yes, your Pie Chart Promoter put you in a 100/0 pie. Follow these steps:

1. Tally up the before-bear-market dollar amount of your portfolio.
2. Subtract 57 percent from it. That's the amount the bear left you in your portfolio.

During that bear market, you lost 57 percent of your whole portfolio, which reduced your $2 million portfolio by $1,140,000. The bear ate well. It left you with $860,000.

What if you were in a blended 60/40 pie chart? Let's look at what happened to the exchange-traded funds (ETFs) typically used in these plans from December 31, 2021, to October 12, 2022:

- SPDR S&P 500 ETF (SPY): -24.95 percent
- Lehman Brothers Aggregate Bond ETF (AGG): -17.93 percent

So the 60 percent portion lost 24.95 percent of its value, and the 40 percent portion lost 17.93 percent (I'll explain this second calculation in a minute), which gives you a total portfolio return of -22.14 percent.

Read that again. *That's a true bear market loss for the 60/40 model.* That's your painful story. Both parts of your pie lost money.

Remember that magicians use misdirection to distract you. Those Pie Chart Promoter magicians want to distract you from your pain by telling you the 40 percent portion is made of "safe" investments. You've just seen the lie.

You lost tons of money you can no longer spend because the bear ate it. And the bear ate very well. Your advisor should be (at the very least) ashamed. They should train for a different profession.

It's all due to the sequence-of-returns risk and a Pie Chart Promoter who never listened to you and never did the job. I'm sure they never told you that at age sixty-five on October 10, 2007, the stock market was going to crater 57 percent over seventeen months. No one told you that. But your advisor didn't protect you from it, either.

Time to Recover from Being Mauled by the Bear

Take a pencil and a straightedge to draw lines on your Page 4 Chart. It's pretty easy. You take the top of the bear market and the top of the bull market. So on October 10, 2007, you draw a straight horizontal line, and then you say to yourself, okay, what's the exact date? Where does the S&P 500 reach this line again?

We've had twenty-two bear markets since 1925. Track all those highs to the lows and then draw a straight line from the high. Then calculate the day it gets back to where it was from the prior high. And that becomes your "time to recover" or "break-even" statistic. And then you take all of those times-to-recover statistics and average them.

That's how I got those average break-even times you see in table 3 (chapter 2) . That's how I know it took from October 10, 2007, to March 22, 2013—five years, five months, and twelve days—to get back to break-even after the Great Recession. You do that calculation after every single bear market, and you get the numbers in the table.

Now, the vast majority of sophisticated, seasoned investors probably understand that. I would be willing to say the vast majority of investing novices, as I call them, go to one of the major household-name financial services firms. They fill out the famous risk tolerance questionnaire that everybody in my industry has.

If the advisor doesn't like your score, they'll call you up. I guarantee this: They won't like your score when it doesn't correspond to what their firm's policies *allow them* to invest you in. What if you're "full steam ahead" for a 100/0, saying, "Risks? Who cares? Let's make money!" What if you're a twenty-one-year-old internet multimillionaire (which those advisors don't know yet because only a pretty person in the lobby or the 800 hotline guy has spoken to you)? They give you the same nonsense I mentioned earlier for fifty-five-year-old Mrs. Jefferson. That Pie Chart Promoter of an advisor will swear up and down that they can't give you what you want.

Run. What are you waiting for? Run!

No "assigned pie chart allocation" suits you when you barely survived the last bear market. No pie chart suits you when you want your money manager to manage you away from the bear.

AGG vs. S&P 500

Now, I promised to tell you how I arrived at the loss numbers for the 40 percent portion of your portfolio in that earlier section. When we looked at your 60/40 portfolio losses in a -57 percent bear market, the 40 percent portion was clearly not protected. How do we know?

When we talk about people getting clobbered by bear markets, there are two things worth mentioning. If you were in a 100/0 plan, then you took the entire -57 percent hit to your face. If you were in a 60/40 plan, then 60 percent of your money was hit by the -57 percent.

That 60 percent of your investments is defined by the S&P 500.

The 40 percent in that allocation is not part of the S&P 500, so where is it? We need the sandbox behind the second number in the asset allocation. If you're in an 80/20, 60/40, 40/60, or 20/80 plan, there has to be a product that defines what that second number is in your asset allocation model.

The most commonly used product is the AGG. The AGG is the Lehman Brothers Aggregate Bond Index. I think of it as the first cousin to the S&P 500 index. The S&P 500 is for stocks, while the AGG is for bonds. That 40 percent of your investments is defined by the AGG.

Remember, the S&P 500 index has an official history going back to 1957, with testing back to 1925. The AGG goes back to only 2003, as you see in figure 4.[54] Since the AGG didn't exist until 2003, and to make it all fit with the S&P 500, the candlesticks in the chart are calendar quarters. The thin red line is the S&P 500, and you can see that it skyrockets well above the AGG.

Figure 4. AGG and S&P 500 (2000-25)

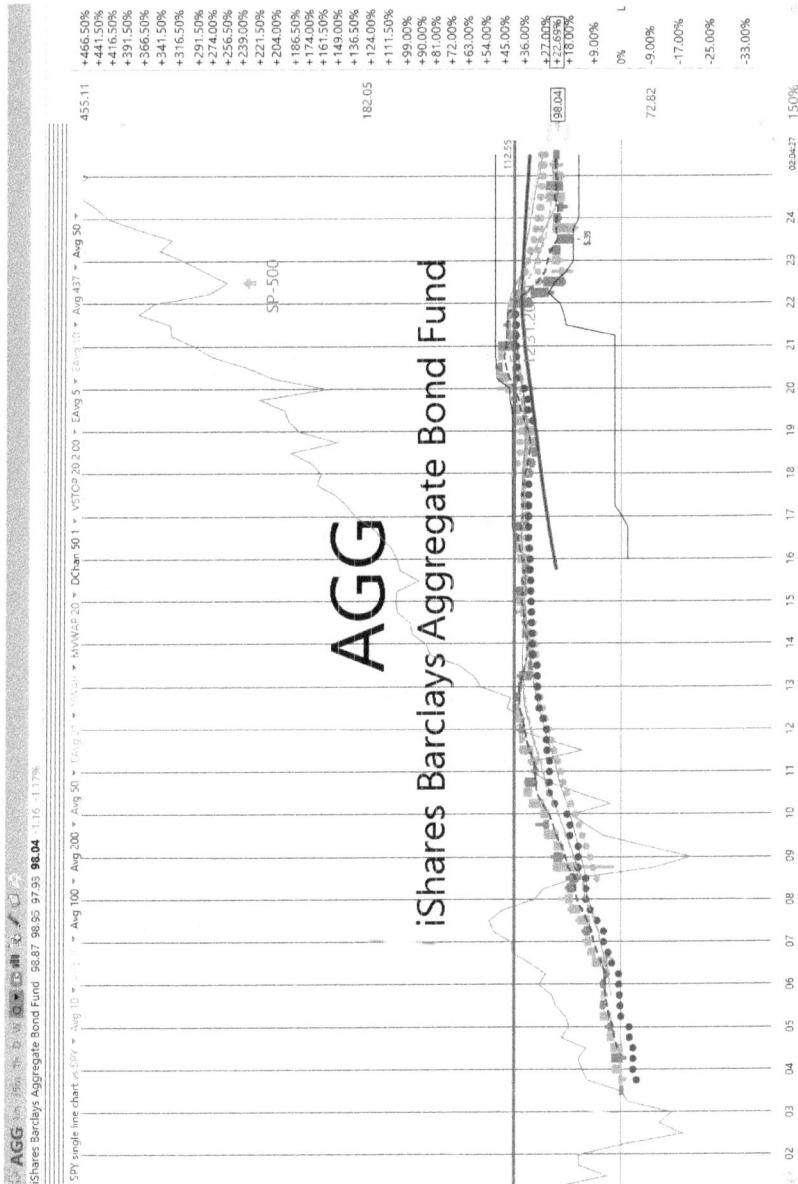

Chart provided by TC2000®

Take a look at this chart. The AGG has been pretty pathetic since the end of 2021—flat, flat, flat. In 2003, it was at $80, and right now it's $97. So from 2003 to today, it's gained $17 on a denominator of $80. So in round numbers, it's gained 21 percent in twenty-two years. That's less than 1 percent per year, a truly pathetic return.

Now, here's another denial. The AGG has had some really big negative years, and nobody wants to talk about this because they just don't want to talk about bad news. Advisors who put you in this piece of their pie chart sold it to you as "protection." They are unmistakably dead wrong, as we have mathematically demonstrated. That's why they never say this out loud. You can see that every advisor active since 2003 *knows* how pathetic the results have been. They can read a chart. You can read a chart. They avoid talking about the chart.

Let me break the math down in a different way.

The AGG fell from $114 to $94 between December 31, 2021, and October 20, 2022. This means when you want to know the losses on the 40 percent portion of the 60/40 blend, you're going to use a decline of $114 over $94. That's -17.5 percent—a significant number! Even if you were 0/100, with nothing in the S&P 500 and 100 percent in the AGG for the last twenty-two years, it *looks like* you've made 21 percent on your money. But that's an aggregate return for twenty-two years. That doesn't reflect compounding. If we take twenty-two years and ask what the compound yearly rate of return is to that positive 21 percent, it's going to be something like 0.84 percent. Your total return is . . . laughable.

Let's look at the AGG numbers:

AGG price on December 31, 2021: $114

AGG price on October 22, 2023: $94

Portfolio allocation: 40 percent in AGG

What does this give you?

Step 1: Calculate Percentage Loss for AGG

$$\$114 - \$94 = \$20$$
$$\$20/\$114 = -17.54\%$$

Step 2: Calculate Portfolio Impact

$$40\% \times -17.54\% = -7.02\%$$

Here's the naked truth: If you're in a 60/40 model, you're bringing in 60 percent of a negative number and 40 percent of a negative number. There's no escaping it. The bear eats you.

Now, maybe some brokerage firm has something different from the AGG. Maybe Morgan Stanley and Wells Fargo or the others have their in-house bond models. But the vast majority of investment advisors use the AGG.

It's sad. The AGG has beaten the S&P 500 only four or five times in its history. When the S&P 500 fell 57 percent from October 2007 to March 2009, the AGG beat that for five years.

It's undeniable. The AGG is a very sad chart. So if you're in that 60/40 blend, you're in pretty bad shape because you're getting 40 percent of 0.66 percent. And guess what? It brought in half of that today, May 27, 2025. Right now, as I write this, the AGG is at 0.32 percent today, and 0.66 percent year-to-date. If you go back to last Friday's close, the AGG was at 0.33 percent. Now you're getting 40 percent of 0.33 percent. Why? Because the S&P 500 year-to-date (January 1–May 27, 2025) is 0.33 percent, but only because it's up 1.54 percent today. So if you want last Friday's close, you take 0.33 percent and subtract 1.54 percent. Let me repeat that: The S&P 500 has earned 0.33 percent year-to-date because it gained 1.55 percent *just today*.

Look at the Page 4 Chart. What was the bear market decline in 2022 on the S&P 500? It was -25 percent between January 3 and October 12, 2022. So now we're going to multiply -25 percent by 0.6 percent. That's 15 percent. The 60 percent portion loses 15 percent. The 40 percent portion loses 7.2 percent. In all, your 60/40 model came in at 22.2 percent.

Let me point this out once again: None of the firms I have been talking about put this scary stuff on their websites. Nowhere on those websites are you going to find that on October 12, 2022, your 60/40 blend was -22.2 percent.

As you can see, nothing is exciting about the 40 percent side of the 60/40 blend. The AGG year-to-date in 2025 is 0.66 percent.

Do you really need to put 40 percent of your wealth into AGG with such returns?

Myth: Bonds Down, Stocks Up

You've perhaps heard, "When the stock market goes down, the bond market goes up." Then your advisor tells you, "You'll be fine."

People talk about that relationship like it's the truth in all cases. No. It is a gross misrepresentation that, generally speaking (with huge emphasis on the word *generally*), when stocks go up, bonds go down. That is a generally accepted narrative. It is not true at least half the time.

All you have to do is look at the chart for the 2003 calendar year. Take all of 2003 to 2025, that's twenty-three and a half years (we're only halfway through 2025). If you look at those twenty-three years and ask how many times bonds beat the S&P 500, it's a total of five. So for five out of twenty-three or so years, bonds beat the S&P 500. Only five. The other eighteen times, bonds went down and the S&P 500 went up.

Bonds up and stocks down is thus debunked by the very charts recording their respective historic movements. That's what a recent news article from Bloomberg was about. It claimed bonds had bounced back in response to positive trade news. Trump had just extended the European Union tariff increase deadline to July 9. Bloomberg's head-line on May 27, 2025, was "Stocks Gain on Trade Talks as Treasuries Rally: Markets Wrap."[55] The reason I sent it to everybody is that it talks about how this news affected the

60/40 blend. It's timely in two ways: It talks first about why stocks rallied (the tariff deadline extension) and then about how it was positive for the bond markets (a.k.a. the 60/40 portfolio blend).

11
INSANITY, DOUBLED

I rail against the buy-and-hold approach because of its double insanity. It's not only American investors but their money managers who jump off tall buildings due to losses made in a dramatic bear market.

Advisors Lose Too: Double Insanity

This is not well known, but advisors lose in a bear market, too, not just you. When markets fall, client portfolio values drop, so the dollar amount of the advisor's fee (calculated as a percentage of the total assets under management) also declines.

In a bear market, total assets shrink. The industry doesn't want you to know much about that. But now you do.

Let me share with you some very simple real-life math. The S&P 500 was down 57 percent as of March 6, 2009. For simplicity, say you're the advisor and 100 percent of your clients own the S&P 500. Also say zero clients leave you. Your assets under management (all the money your clients entrust to you to manage) drop 57 percent. Your fee billings are also -57 percent.

Let's say that, along the way from -1 percent to -57 percent, clients outright leave you. Your assets under management and your fee billings are now worse than -57 percent.

Now, say you work for a giant financial services company whose name everyone recognizes. It goes bankrupt and the Secretary of the Treasury orders Bank of America to buy it. You're a whole lot worse off than -57 percent. So -57 percent is only a baseline for the actual damages.

There are a lot of dead bodies on both sides of the aisle. Clients have lost fortunes, but there are investment advisors and stockbrokers who have committed suicide. I won't even hazard a guess as to what led them to do so.

Are Advisors Bailing Out? Yes and No

The question must be asked: Why the devil aren't advisors making a change in their own favor, even if they're not considering the client?

They are. Some of them are.

There's a newsletter, Advisor Hub, that tracks recruiting by industry. Its headline on May 12, 2025, was "Sanctuary Snags Florida-Based UBS Team Managing $2 Billion."[56] Its opening paragraph states, "A 12-person UBS Wealth Management USA team overseeing around $2 billion in client assets across offices in Florida, Ohio and South Carolina has left to join independent broker-dealer and advisory firm Sanctuary Wealth." It was not the only migration from UBS to other firms between April and May, either.

Why has Charles Schwab become the biggest in the world? Charles Schwab has eighteen thousand advisors. I'm on the recruiting side, and the business development officers at Schwab all know who I am. Once or twice a month, I'll get a phone call or an email saying something like, "Jack, I'm dealing with Mr. JB at Merrill Lynch. He wants to move to Schwab. He wants to talk to somebody who went through it. Can you talk to him and share your experience?" I do it, of course. No problem. Most of the time, it's someone from LPL, the biggest independent broker-dealer. By "independent," I mean they're not owned by an insurance company or a bank. LPL is publicly traded and is the biggest independent broker-dealer. Charles Schwab is the biggest independent custodian.

Charles Schwab legally has to be a broker-dealer (executing trades for clients), but its real function is custodial, to hold and safeguard client assets. Like Costco, which supplies goods in bulk to members, Schwab provides custodial, trading, technology, and operational services to thousands of independent, fee-based advisors (registered investment advisors, or RIAs). It provides a platform. Charles Schwab doesn't promote mutual funds or variable annuities.

I've publicly said this at seminars: To the best of my knowledge, Schwab has never lied to me. Schwab has never misled me, and I've been with them for over fourteen years.

I have zero complaints. I can't tell you anything that Charles Schwab has ever done wrong or done to disappoint me. It's been a perfect relationship.

Advisors are of two minds:

1. Some are locked into their current narrative as the only way to do things: sell in-house products, do buy-and-hold, and use the pie chart model. They are passive or non-managers of their clients' money.

2. Some are not willing to be Pie Chart Promoters anymore, as their firms insist, and they depart. That's how Schwab has come to have many more advisors than other organizations.

Why do advisors leave those companies and join Charles Schwab? Simple: They want to be fee-based and independent. They're angry and frustrated and stressed out. They're tired of vice presidents giving them a hard time every day and threatening their jobs because they didn't sell enough of the ABC mutual fund. They have to meet the quota for the ABC fund because it gave the firm a $250,000 check to support a convention. They can't invest, protect, and grow their clients' wealth in the *other ways* that are out there.

That's the reality in the big brokerage firms that the public doesn't know about. If you're with *any* broker who calls you up and says, "You need to take a position in the ABC fund," be very wary. Be aware that it sure as hell isn't because the ABC fund is the top performer. It's because a product manager inside the broker's organization is pushing them to hit a quota for the ABC fund.

Some 99 percent of the public doesn't have a clue that this phenomenon exists or realize the extent to which it's part of the problem. Well, you do now. You learned it here.

Your Money Doesn't Have to Be the Bear's Lunch

I called out the bear markets using the Page 4 Chart. It's scary because the average American investor doesn't understand this strong buy-side bias. I hope you understand it better now. I do hope you see the downsides of letting an advisor put you in a pie chart and use only a buy-and-hold strategy.

My firm, RFS, has a buy-sell approach. We do what works to increase and protect our clients' wealth. You probably understand by now that we are not buy-and-hold in all cases at RFS. (While I've been hinting about it, I'll get more into our strategy for our clients in parts 3 and 4.)

All those big advisory firms want you to believe they're investor-friendly. They want you to believe they're protecting your money. And that narrative might be partially true. The top brokerage firms are, after all, what many investors expect and stay with, which is how they all got so big.

I want you to expect something better. I want you to expect that the bear won't eat you alive. I want you to expect that you're protected from the sequence-of-returns risk.

Here's the part of the story that isn't jumping out at you from any of those big firms' websites: They are all for-profit corporations. They make money through the fees they charge clients. They make more fees on stock funds than they do on bond and money market funds.

So not only did the big advisory firms drink the Kool-Aid but Fidelity in particular (my opinion, as it's the oldest kid on the block) invented the Kool-Aid. Fidelity invented the buy-and-hold Kool-Aid. Fidelity wants you to be an aggressive growth investor. Why? Because when you own Fidelity *stock* funds, they make more money than when you own Fidelity *bond* funds. The fact is that stock funds have a higher expense ratio (fees for them) than bond funds. Bond funds have a higher expense ratio than money market funds. Don't let a Pie Chart Promoter line their pockets with fees when you're losing your shirt. Expect and get better.

PART THREE
YOU EAT THE BEAR

Photo credit: iStock.com/jhorrocks

I showed you my firm's results during those bear markets. Your money can achieve those results too. The bear doesn't need to gobble up your wealth. The bear doesn't need to be allowed to eat up all the past gains your investments have earned you.

But you can't achieve this while sitting in a pie chart. You can't do it with a buy-and-hold strategy. You can't do it with passivity.

According to Cerulli Associates' data,[57] these are the most important objectives cited by the affluent when they hire advisors:

1. Wealth preservation (72 percent)
2. Tax preservation (63 percent)
3. Wealth transfer strategies (48 percent)
4. Risk management (44 percent)
5. Income generation (35 percent)

Do you see how buying and holding during a bear market wipes out the number one objective of the affluent investor? There is no wealth preservation with buy-and-hold.

Here in part 3, I'll be doing some more debunking of the current narrative. You need knowledge of what so many advisors are doing wrong with those two all-important wealth preservation and risk management objectives. Only then can you move on to doing things the right way.

I'll also be giving you some clues about how to interview a financial advisor who is a fiduciary. That's a professional with your best interests at heart and not their own.

12
DATA-DRIVEN,
DATA-PROVEN STATEMENTS

I think at this point, you will now see a red flag waving as if it's in a gale force wind when you see the Page 4 Chart declines but hear your advisor say, "Just be patient. It will bounce back. It's just a small correction."

You know how to run the other way with your money. You know that your buy-and-hold advisor has no wealth protection strategy for you in a market "correction." You know there's potentially a big, hungry bear racing toward you to gobble up your wealth.

Your advisor keeps saying, "We don't have a crystal ball, but we have history: The markets always rise again. They always bounce back."

What you can never know is *when*. When will they bounce back to break even and start earning again? Go back to my charts of break-even times in chapter 3. Will it take two months this time? Two years? Thirteen years?

You need better protection.

Now, let me say this. Over time talking with investing novices, I've understood that this is not well known. Your advisor charges you a percentage fee for something you can get for free. It's called VOO.

VOO is the ticker symbol for the Vanguard S&P 500 ETF, an exchange-traded fund. It aims to closely track the performance of the S&P 500, which represents five hundred of the largest US companies.

By investing in VOO, investors gain exposure to the US stock market through one highly liquid security. I say it again: Any investor can do this all on their own. There's no need to consult or pay an advisor. You can do it if you want diversification across major sectors and industries.

But advisors don't tell you this. Too many of them take your money and invest in VOO for you. For a fee. Sure, they're following their financial firm's protocols. In my opinion, over 80 percent of investors are being completely screwed over by those protocols. Why are you paying a 1 percent management fee when your investment advisor is a Pie Chart Promoter who lost over half your money in 2007–09? You're paying somebody to put your money into the next potential -57 percent. If you wanted to lose 57 percent, you could do it all on your own just by investing in the VOO.

It's not against the law for these advisors to do this. As I see it, though, it's highly unethical. The industry pros don't call it unethical, and certainly not even "ineffective," much less "dubious," but why put up with it? It's like going to Macy's and paying five hundred dollars for the exact branded product that's three hundred dollars at Costco.

I think you understand my position by now. You don't have to be one of those people who are paying a management fee to lose 49 percent, 57 percent, 34 percent, or 25 percent. Just look at J.P. Morgan's Page 4 Chart. Look at it again and again to remind yourself of what you're avoiding by *not* doing things the Pie Chart Promoter way.

No Human Alive

Let's recall some information I've given you and look at some new data.

S&P 500

You know the S&P 500 has officially been in existence since 1957. If you invested $100 in it at the beginning of 1957, you would have about $90,932.85 at the end of 2025 (not adjusting for inflation). This is assuming you reinvested all dividends and withdrew none of that money. It's a return on investment of 90,832.85 percent. That gives you an annual return of 10.47 percent. When it's adjusted for inflation, we have an average annual *real* return of 6.6 percent.[58]

I grant you this: The only problem with the S&P 500 Page 4 Charts that J.P. Morgan publishes every month is that they go back to only 1997. Yes, the S&P 500 officially came into existence in 1957, so there is prior data. And the stock market certainly existed before the official S&P 500 came to be.

A very famous Wharton professor, Jeremy Siegel, has data from which he estimated what the S&P 500 would have looked like back to 1925 and even 1802. Siegel went out on a limb, statistically speaking, and wrote a famous book called *Stocks for the Long Run*. He used historical data from various sources to estimate the performance of a broad stock market index going back to 1802. That's an academic stretch, an estimate, but nonetheless, he did it. My point? We have a lot of data.

Data before 1925 is very sketchy because of fires. Since 1925, from very reliable data, there have been twenty-two bear markets (remember: a decline of over 20 percent) in ninety-nine years. I don't count this year, 2025, as it's still in progress.

QQQ

The QQQ is the NASDAQ's 100 largest technology stocks. In this market, there is no 500 equivalent to the S&P 500. Since the launch of QQQ in March 1999 through June 13, 2025, it's up approximately 1,115.9 percent on a total return basis.[59] This includes reinvested dividends.

VOO

Vanguard launched the VOO in September 2010. It's up approximately 612.5 percent on a total return basis (including dividends reinvested) as of June 13, 2025.[60]

To understand the distinction between the two terms I'll be presenting in the next section, we have to appreciate one fact. No human alive has been invested in the S&P 500 since 1957 in a continuous, uninterrupted manner. Let's define what I mean. There is no single individual who put money into the S&P 500 in 1957 and never touched that money again, never withdrew a penny, and never added another penny to the account. There's no one out there who invested a given sum in the QQQ on Day 1 and left it there untouched. I would put my hand in the fire about it.

But the "big total returns" I described a moment ago, such as a 6.6 percent real annual return, are what your advisor would like you to believe you can earn with their buy-and-hold strategy. Don't believe it. Take your money and run the other direction.

Now, let's look at two terms that advisors love to suppress. They're pretty successful at it because they've got enormous advertising budgets and enormous power that comes from throwing that money around.

Investor Returns vs. Investment Returns

Look up the difference between *investor return* and *investment return*. You'll read something like the following:

> *Investment return* is how much an investment
> (including price changes and any dividend
> income paid) gives you over a period. This is,
> however, assuming that you, the investor, hold the
> investment throughout that period.

It's your theoretical return. We've discussed how, in its
history, the S&P 500 has risen. Over time, over decades, the
trend line is bullish. It goes up. We all hear that. We can take
a "lifetime chart" and see that by drawing with a pencil and
a straightedge from left to right on the chart.

You now also know this: "The market always bounces
back" is the buy-and-hold guys' mantra in every "correction."
This is their mantra in every full-blown, -20 percent bear
market. Now . . .

> *Investor return* is the actual return that you earn
> on your investment account. It takes into account
> your buying and selling decisions, the cash you
> put into and take out of the account during
> the period.

This is your actual, money-in-your-pocket return. It's
nothing like the investment return. This is the return that
accounts for the fact that the market is a pool—a great big
swimming pool.

Cash Flow Makes Those Returns a Lie: Cash Flows Distort

Back to that "buy-and-hold on—the market always moves higher" nonsense. There are no living humans to prove an investor always comes out positive in the long run. The stock market is a giant swimming pool. You have people getting into investments with new money every day. You have people getting their money out every day. I have clients who have been with me continuously since 1992. I have clients who can show thirty-three years of investment returns with me.

The investor return is not the investment return.

Cash flows—pulling money out and putting money into your investments—distort investment returns. When you're adding and removing money, you're distorting your returns. But lots of investors take money out of their investment accounts. You want to buy cars or a house, pay college tuition, or buy a new furnace for the house. They get money ahead, and they get back into the S&P pool with new funds. In and out. That's the nature of money, investing, and markets.

By making those perfectly acceptable deposits and withdrawals, you distort that return. And that's not in the investment track record. The investment track record doesn't talk about cash flows. Not only would we have to find somebody who's owned the S&P 500 since their very first deposit but that person has to be able to show that they've never added money or taken money out of their account. Otherwise, we can't equate the investment return to the investor's return. People don't understand that. Their advisors don't tell them.

Every day, people get out of that S&P pool. This "investor return versus investment return" contrast and continuing narrative was irritating a guy (as the much-circulated, but probably fictitious, story goes). He was so irritated that he had to get the data to figure it all out. He apparently wrote to Vanguard, Fidelity, Oppenheimer, Bank of America, Merrill Lynch—all the money managers in the country. He reportedly said, "I have one question. The S&P 500 is at 10.33 percent nominally and 6.47 percent after inflation since 1957. Do you have any living human beings as clients who have continuously owned the S&P 500 for, say, fifty years?"

Nobody wrote back. So all this pie chart talk about the S&P 500 earning 6.47 percent for the last half-century has one big omission. It's the no-living-human argument.

Yes, there may be seniors who have officially been invested in the markets for that long. But remember the getting in/out of the pool aspect of how they manage and use their money. They haven't stayed in the S&P 500 consistently for fifty years; they've been in and out. They haven't had that 6.4 percent positive return.

The Pie Chart Promoters are quoting a track record that has no basis in real life.

There's one more hitch to their argument. The average investor does the second-dumbest thing they could do. They lose 57 percent from October 9, 2007, to March 9, 2009. What do they do (remember how I mentioned fear as a reason not to stay in the market)? They sell everything. Then they end up being out of the market when it rebounds.

13

WHERE TO GET WEALTH-PRESERVING, WEALTH-BUILDING MANAGEMENT

When others report that 89–94 percent of advisors are buy-and-hold Pie Chart Promoters, you know one thing: They're not going to do anything to protect you. If you want to call what those advisors suffer from a herd mentality, that's fine. They're one and the same.

I just find that 89–94 percent to be an amazingly shocking statistic. Let's take airplane pilots. What would happen if 89 percent, much less 94 percent of them, said, "If there are high mountains in my path within the next two minutes, I'd fly into the mountains. No, I wouldn't rise above or go around them. Of course I wouldn't!" We'd have a lot of dead people. Same with surgery and 89–94 percent of surgeons. Same with engineers and bridges or skyscrapers. And on and on.

Here's my problem with that advisor study. Maybe herd mentality has a place (somewhere . . .), but in my industry, it flies in the face of common sense. It negates the promise we make to act in our clients' best interest. It makes a lie of all those website promises that we "protect and grow your wealth," and oh, I boil when I read that.

When you hire a lawyer, a doctor, a surgeon, a plumber, an electrician, you expect them to actively assess the problem. You expect them to fix it in an expert manner—or send you to another type of specialist. You don't expect them to ignore the problem or even to misdiagnose it. Isn't that why we hire professionals?

I don't care whether it's blue-collar tradesmen or licensed doctors and lawyers. You're hiring a professional because you expect them to actively manage the situation that you have brought to their attention. You expect them to come up with a solution. That is the common-sense expectation we all have when hiring a professional.

I've written this book largely for investing novices, whether you've ever hired a financial advisor or not. Now you know the bad news. In my industry, at least 89 percent of professionals are going to do nothing to protect you from the mauling claws of those hungry bears. Those advisors think this is normal. If you lost big in any recent bear market, your advisor was sitting back, drinking the buy-and-hold Kool-Aid.

You know that old definition of insanity? Insanity is repeating the same process over and over and expecting different results. I just don't get why advisors insist on buy-and-hold. After all (as you also now know), they suffer a decrease in earnings, too.

How to Interview a Financial Advisor

I'm going to give you one simple technique to interview any financial advisor. I don't care if they're a Chartered Financial Analyst®. I don't care if they work for a "prestigious" brokerage firm. I don't care if your uncle George recommended you talk to them. I don't care if you ran into them at some Friday night seminar.

The technique is show and tell. You show the investment advisor you are interviewing a printout of the J.P. Morgan Page 4 Chart. I encourage you to print out the most current one from that website. Then, you look them right in the eyes and ask, "Can you show me in writing what you did during the five most recent official bear markets? They are here, here, here, here, and here on this chart. What did you do to protect your clients' money? How well did it go?"

Don't be aggressive. Don't be confrontational. Just use your "I'm really curious" voice.

The simple fact of the matter is, if you want to piss off an investment advisor—89 percent of them—you show them Page 4. You make them prove to you in writing what they did during those five most recent negative bear markets *to protect their clients' money.*

Just let them talk. Or sputter. Or say nothing and turn red. Or start protesting as they shove you out of their office.

If you're both still sitting there and they gave you an answer, then you continue. You demand three references. You need those. Any advisor worth their salt has a good enough relationship with at least three of their clients that they can give you those references. They will have asked for those clients' permission well in advance. That's what an advisor should expect to have to do with any prospective client sitting across from them in the conference room.

No answers to those questions? No references? Move on to the next advisor. Rinse and repeat. If they're not lying, and if you don't do that, then you're not doing *your* due diligence.

You would do that if you were hiring a cataract surgeon, right? I mentioned this exact analogy to a client one day. He perked up and said to me, "You know, Jack, I did that. My insurance company sent me to one cataract surgeon who wanted to schedule me right away. Just the one. But I wanted to interview him. And you know what he told me? For the last 250 surgeries he performed, no patients asked him any questions about his surgical skill or history."

You see? You would do that if you were going to be cut open by a surgeon (and they welcome the opportunity like all *honest* financial advisors do). But you don't check the track record of the advisor.

Don't get caught giving your entire lifetime of wealth to a person who has no track record and no references. Don't work with anyone who is not going to actively protect and grow your money. Don't work with an advisor who, on top of it all, is going to sell you something that you can get for free.

I do respond when people ask me these two questions: "What do we do to protect wealth in a bear market?" and "Can I speak to three of your clients?" The problem? People don't ask me these questions. That's why I proactively bring out that Page 4 Chart. I reveal my firm's results for clients in relation to each bear market on the chart, as I did in chapter 1 for you in this book. I ask my prospective clients straight-up if they would like to speak to two or three of my established clients.

Far too many people with money don't interview the individuals they're handing hundreds of thousands and millions of dollars over to. And, rest assured, this applies to the very affluent as well. No one asks.

I talked about insanity earlier in this chapter, and this is an additional example of the insanity you have to get away from. Interview your advisor!

People who become our clients don't pay my firm because what we do is super secret. The tools, strategies, and processes we use are not top secret at all. Clients pay us because what we do is obscenely time consuming. What do we do? You know it by now: active management, technical analysis, wealth protection, and growth.

I promised you this book wouldn't be heavily technical, and it isn't. Not really. But when I sit with a prospective client, I do more. I give them examples of the technical analysis that many people on my team do all day, every day. My clients get it. It's an advanced skill. It uses advanced software. It's very time consuming. And they are just not in the market to learn it themselves. They know that, and they hire us to do it.

Table 6 is the same one I gave you back in chapter 1, with the most recent bear added. This is the table I give clients along with the Page 4 Chart, and it's why clients hire my firm. We provide much, much happier numbers.

Table 6. Bear Market Performance: RFS vs. the S&P 500

The Bear	The S&P 500	My Firm, RFS
2000–02 dot-com crash	-49%	+13%
2007–09 mortgage & financial crisis	-57%	-4%
2020 pandemic	-34%	-1%
2022 bear market	-25%	-5%
February 19– April 8, 2025	-19.00%	(not an official bear market, but a close call)

14
TAKE YOUR WEALTH AWAY FROM THE PIE CHART PROMOTERS

As I began to write this, the odds were pretty good that we were at the beginning of bear market twenty-three. It didn't happen, as you saw in my table above. Things turned around, and now, mid-July 2025, we're bullish.

But imagine we had sunk into a bear market, into -20 percent or deeper. What would you have been able to do when you were with an advisor who is a buy-and-hold Pie Chart Promoter? Nothing. Nothing except to file a complaint at FINRA.

I'm going to tell you a story from about four years ago. It's about a guy who's on my referral list. This is a fascinating story, and his is not the only one. I've had this happen twenty to twenty-five times.

I got a phone call from a guy I'll call "Jay X." He said, "Jack, my name's Jay X. I'm Jim C's friend and work companion. I've known him for twenty-five years. I need a new investment advisor. He says to call you cause you're the best and you've done a great job. What do I need to do?"

I said, as usual, "Well, I do appreciate that endorsement from Jim C. I still need to take five minutes and walk you through who we are, what we do, and what the process is."

Then and there, I put up Page 4 on our shared conference call screen.

I said, "You're looking at the twenty-eight-year history of bear markets."

He replied, "I've never seen that before. I know what you're talking about, though, because that's the reason I called. That kind of loss happened to me, but it didn't happen to Joe."

We chatted some more. He said, "I'm ready to do paperwork to work with you, but I have a problem. I've been speaking with another investment advisor. I promised him I would let him explain to me what he does before I make a decision."

I liked that he was shopping around. "Jay, by all means, keep that appointment. But I want you to print out what I just showed you."

He got the page online. Then I helped him out. "With that next advisor, you want to begin the conversation with a couple of questions. First, you say, 'Here's J.P. Morgan's famous Page 4. Can you prove to me what your investment return was during all five of these corrections?' Then you say, 'Oh, and can you give me three names of longtime clients of yours?'"

I heard the outcome later. Jay's meeting with the guy was a Zoom call. He put the chart up on the screen, and the investment advisor got really cross and hung up on him!

The first thing I tell everybody is that I don't chase people. I get referrals. I'm in some networks. Word gets out.

It can also happen like this: I'm at the pool, and the next-door neighbor says, "You have a really nice house. What do you do for a living?"

I tell him, "I'm a fiduciary fee-based investment advisor, and Charles Schwab is our primary custodian. I help people manage their money. We also do deep financial planning and retirement income projections."

Then I hit him with the super-soft close. "If you'd like, we give everybody a no-obligation free interview. So anytime you want to, you can come over to my house and we'll sit down together behind my screen and I'll show you how I work. Case in point, back in 2020, the S&P 500 was -34 percent. Do you remember that terrible bear market?"

He does.

"Did you get hurt?"

He makes a face. "Of course. I got really hurt. Everybody got hurt."

I go on. "No disrespect intended, but that's not the truth. Not everybody got hurt when the S&P 500 was -34 percent. My clients were only at -1 percent. I'm willing to show you for free how I did that."

He jumps on it. "When I get back from Detroit, we'll sit down."

And the very first thing I begin that conversation with is Page 4.

The Page 4 Chart Signals

On April 8, 2025, the S&P 500 was negative, just tenths of a point above -20 percent. We were staring at our bear market. It would have taken a drop of just one more percentage point to put us there. It didn't happen, as we all now know from the data. That's why on my Page 4 Chart highlights, I just call out the potential bear (that yellow highlight with no percentage in it).

If I had been ready to publish my book then, that Page 4 Chart and my discussion of it would have been very different.

Here I am, though, in mid-July 2025. What has happened since early April? Page 4 shows us how we snapped back, and today we're 100 percent in a bull market buy signal.

Is the next big bear market still out there? Is it still a threat? Do you (and your advisors) still need to be on your toes? Sure. Always.

Remember that, statistically, we have bears on average every 4.7 years. That's why you still need to go out and get yourself a money manager who knows what to do to protect you from that next bear. Find someone who not only knows but takes the right actions. No buy-and-hold will do for you ever again.

I don't trust politicians or cable news talking heads. I trust *The Wall Street Journal* but not Wall Street. By "Wall Street" I mean the big boys of finance, the big brokerage firms. The prevailing narrative on Wall Street is not the truth. Statistically, I believe I've proven they're not telling the truth.

People are paying a management fee for something they are not receiving. The big boys, those large financial advisory firms, get away with it. Why? Because they have, in a sense, written their own rules, and over the decades, everyone has just come to accept them without scrutiny. For the regulatory authorities to wake up, find you, and sanction you, you or your firm has to have done something really bad.

There is a rule system with the Securities and Exchange Commission (SEC), yes. The rules are really laws that, notably, prohibit fraudulent activities and require market transparency. There are more, but these two are flouted far too often.

I believe the rule system is very misleading. Whenever you have one of these bear markets, the word all over the financial press from *investors* is "Nobody told me this could happen. I didn't know this could happen. Nobody told me I could lose 20 percent." That's because no one did tell them! This is neither a truthful way of doing business nor market transparency.

One of the reality checks I give people is, "Do you know you could lose 20–40 percent, or even over half of your money?"

They systematically respond, "No, nobody told me that. My broker never told me. My advisor never talks about losses."

Advisors don't lie—not exactly. They omit the truth. They never tell a client they're protecting their money from the bear. They can't. It's a lie. So they push "Hang on. We'll hold through the storm. You'll be fine."

Remember chapter 10 and the 60/40 model. It's an illusion. We did the math in chapter 10. Is your 40 percent performing well when the 60 percent gets eaten by the bear? No, your 60 percent loses. Your 40 percent loses. You lose. You, a trusting investor, are not getting expert management for the fees you pay.

Novice Investors Beware

Say you have a next-door neighbor whose advisors turned his $14 million into $3 million. Yes, you read that correctly. His advisors lost $11 million of his money in 2008. Then he got hit with a margin call. On December 17, 2008, he threw himself under the Shady Grove Metro stop in Gaithersburg, Maryland.[61] Yes, your neighbor killed himself. You're not going to read that story on any financial advisor's website. You might never read the real reason he did it in any media.

If you're a forty-five-year-old schoolteacher and you've been lucky enough to sock $200,000 into your 403(b) and then your plan administrators lose 40 percent of it, you're going to have a psychiatric meltdown.

The lie that "it always bounces back" is being institutionalized. It's being cemented into novice investors' psyches. This is achieved thanks to the billions of dollars in advertising that the big firms in the sector spend. They need to do a hard sell of their buy-and-hold, "it always bounces back" nonsense.

Say you're a journalist. You want to report a story on NASCAR, but you only talk about the guy who won. You talk about how skillful he was. Here's the rub. You didn't mention the two drivers who crashed and died. You were silent about their widows and children. You didn't mention the drivers who were maimed in the same race. Is that omission or is that truthful reporting?

You want the truth, the whole truth, and nothing but the truth. Most advisors haven't even got a clue how to give it to you (and aren't allowed to if they do know).

The King Farm Story

I chat with a number of advisors every year on behalf of Schwab. It was about ten years ago that I chatted with a guy who ended up joining Schwab. Let's call him Stuart. He didn't join me and my team, but I was part of the path that got him to Charles Schwab. He came in from Morgan Stanley.

I asked Stuart, "Why are you leaving Morgan Stanley?"

King Farm in Rockville, Maryland, used to be the biggest dairy farm in Montgomery County back in the 1950s. That was back when dairy trucks delivered milk to your front door. It's now a massively successful, affluent neighborhood. Stuart's Morgan Stanley office was in King Farm.

He said, "The branch manager is a no-show. He's always out playing golf. Every single day, mutual fund wholesalers bring us breakfast and lunch. Yup, five days a week. You know what? About 99 percent of the assets under management in our office are mutual fund pie charts. We're not making money for our clients, and I can't take it anymore."

Now, be aware that I'm just reporting a story here. I took it for what it was at the time, and I do believe it. I believe it because, as I've been saying, this is how our industry works. I've been observing how things happen for a long, long time. I've talked to a lot of advisors, including others telling similar tales. I believe this story.

If I told you this story was from the very tiniest Edward Jones office in a blink-and-you-miss-it backwater town, you would probably shrug. You would say, "Oh, well. That's how they do it at Edward Jones in Blink-and-You-Miss-It, USA." Well, that's not who this is. It's the Morgan Stanley office in the very affluent King Farm, Rockville, Maryland. And 99 percent of all the assets under management are in their mutual fund pie chart. Those funds are from companies that buy them breakfast and lunch every day. How many of their King Farm clients know that—and would be happy if they did?

Investing novices, let me say it again. If your advisor's firm is not willing to tell you not only *how* they increase your wealth but also *how* they protect you from the bears? Grab your money and run the other way. Almost everyone can make you money in a bullish, rising market. You want that, too, of course. But don't let that advisor sin by omission by not talking about the bears.

You need a team watching the markets, the trends, the news, and the technical indicators appearing on those charts. You need them doing this on your behalf all day long. You need them to take action on the technical indicators that say it's time to move. Then, you need them to actually move your money to protect your wealth. This is what our advisors do for each and every one of our clients at Research Financial Strategies.

Put your foot down: No more buy-and-hold. No more pie charts. No more of those Pie Chart Promoters pretending to manage your money while they do *not* protect your wealth and while they do *not* grow your money as well as they could.

I invite you to scour my firm's website, especially our Investment Risk Management page: rfsadvisors.com/investment-risk-management.

PART FOUR
THIS MATH CAGES THE BEAR

Photo credit: iStock.com/jhorrocks

Most investing novices may think there is one market. There's the stock market, and that's it.

But, you've started to see that the market is sliced and diced. It's organized in indexes. You've heard of the S&P 500 because of our Page 4 Chart. There's also the NASDAQ

100, the Wilshire 5000, and the Dow Jones Industrial Average (DJIA). By now you can guess that there are even more. There's the S&P Small-Cap 600, the Russell (Small-Cap) 2000, the S&P Mid-Cap 400 Index, and so on.

To some extent, yes, there is one market for stocks. But in addition to the indexes, there are charts. As you can guess, there's more than just the Page 4 Chart.

It's time to become familiar with some others. Why? To understand how a financial advisor worth their salt goes about protecting your wealth in one of those bear markets. You'll also see how that great advisor grows your wealth.

I won't get too technical, I promise. Once you see the charts I'm going to present in the next chapter or two, you'll be able to have another conversation with your current advisor—one that may make them very, very uncomfortable. That's because they don't believe their clients know anything about what I'm going to tell you.

15
THE ELEVEN CHARTS

I told you CNBC featured an executive from Home Depot in 2024. Remember how he said they talk to their partners (their largest purchasers) all the time? Their partners told them back then that consumers who had money weren't spending it, but not because they didn't have it. They weren't spending it because they were scared.

I'm reminding you because Home Depot is part of a collection of eleven charts we need to look at now. Yes, more slicing and dicing of the stock market.

You might ask, "How many stocks are there, anyway?" Most people just think of "stocks," as I said. The New York Stock Exchange lists about 2,132 stocks, while the NASDAQ lists around 3,767. However, as of early 2025, there were 30,000 publicly traded instruments with ticker symbols. They include stocks, bonds, exchange-traded funds (ETFs), mutual funds, options, futures, commodities, etc.

Depending on the economic sector the business is in, its stock may fall into one of eleven sector groups. I call them the Eleven Charts. Each sector has a ticker symbol to identify it, and the companies in each sector are formed into an ETF.

Novice investors need to understand that there is a process and a skillset that a great advisor will use to rotate your money from one economic sector of stocks (one of the Eleven Charts) into another. This is because not all sectors are rising at the same time. I'll get to that.

Pie Chart Promoters don't do this, as you now know. I told you that money moves, and this is one way it moves—as your savvy, alert, honest advisors roll you out of a negative sector into a positive one.

In the eleven economic sectors, you always want to own companies that are placed in the three at the top. You want the ones that are performing the most positively. The top three sectors aren't always the same, so your money must move to follow them.

This is just more knowledge that those buy-and-hold crews don't have or use in their clients' favor. They certainly don't want you to know this.

Eleven Charts

This isn't nuclear physics; this isn't calculus. It's only a set of eleven charts.

If I were to show an eighth grader the Eleven Charts (and I have—my grandkids get this from me) and say, "Pick the three best," the eighth grader could do that. One of my granddaughters did it when she was six years old.

It takes a couple of minutes to review the charts. Then, anybody with common sense can see which one is the best-performing and which one is the worst of them.

Now what do you do with that information? You own the three best-performing sectors. You buy into those ETFs. At any given point, you want to be invested in the three best.

Here's a lesson for you about how bull markets are defined. Even the television talking heads never reference this. The Page 4 Chart doesn't show this, either. There's no percentage like the one used for bears (more than a 20 percent decline) to define the bulls.

What's the definition of a bull market?

It's when the top three performing sectors are XLK (Technology), XLF (Banking and Finance), and XLY (Consumer Discretionary).

Among all eleven sectors, those are the bullish ones. Why? When you have a low-interest-rate environment, people are more likely to borrow from their bank (XLF) because they can get a low interest rate. People go places and spend money in the XLY sector, like Amazon. They shop XLY and buy toys for their young kids. They go to XLK and buy their own kinds of toys, right? Most consumers put those toys they buy—cars, trucks, trips, electronics, and so on—on an XLF credit card or a home equity line or other loan.

This, then, is a technical definition of a bull market.

When you have a bear market, you can be sure that those same three sectors are in the toilet. XLY, XLK, and XLF will be performing poorly in relation to the remaining eight sectors. You'll be able to see it right on the charts.

What is the definition of a bear market?

It's when the three top-performing sectors are XLU (Utilities), XLP (Consumer Staples), and XLE (Energy). In fact, when XLY, XLK, and XLF have moved to the bottom three positions, that's also the technical definition of a bear market. No matter how bad off you are (unless you're homeless), you're going to pay your utility bills and buy gas. XLP is the needs, the staples, the "paper towel and toilet paper fund." These are basic necessities. Thus, the technical definition of a bear market is that XLU, XLP, and XLE are at the top of the eleven charts as best-performing, while XLK, XLF, and XLY sink to the bottom.

Now that you have those tidbits of new knowledge, let me give you the Eleven Charts as they stand when I'm writing this.[62] How do the bullish charts look versus the bearish ones? Note how some charts I call "sloppy" might (or might not) be transitioning.

First, table 7 shows the eleven sectors. In the next pages, I show a chart of each sector. These charts are your clue to how stocks in those sectors might be doing.

Table 7. Top Stock in Each Sector

Sector Symbol	Top Stock in the Sector	Sector Name
XLB	Linde (LIN)	Materials
XLC	Meta Platforms (META)	Communications
XLE	Exxon Mobil (XOM)	Energy
XLF	Berkshire Hathaway (BRK.B)	Financials
XLI	GE Aerospace (GE)	Industrials
XLK	Microsoft (MSFT)	Information Technology
XLP	Procter & Gamble (PG)	Consumer Staples
XLRE	Prologis (PLD)	Real Estate
XLU	NextEra Energy (NEE)	Utilities
XLV	UnitedHealth Group (UNH)	Healthcare
XLY	Amazon.com (AMZN)	Consumer Discretionary

Figure 5. XLC (Communications)
+11.2488% YTD—Strong Buy Pattern

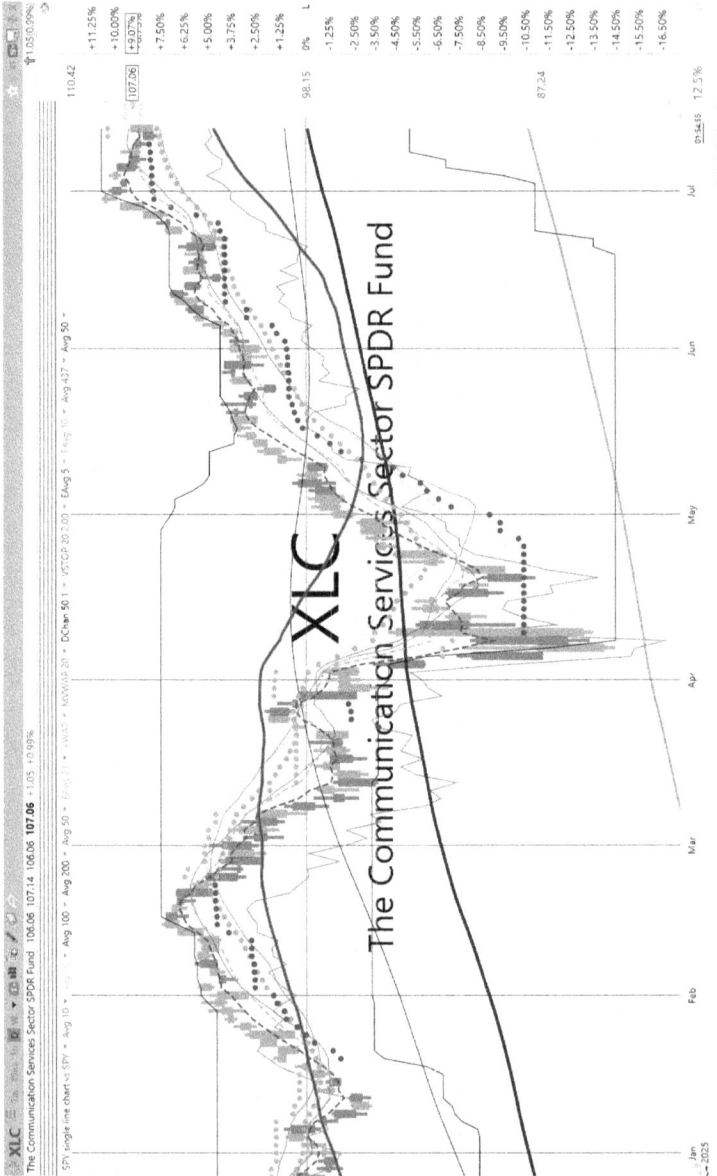

Chart provided by TC2000®

Figure 6. XLF (Financials)
+10.0766% YTD—Very Strong Buy Pattern

Chart provided by TC2000®

Figure 7. XLP (Consumer Staples)
+4.4396% YTD—Sloppy Sideways Pattern, No Buy

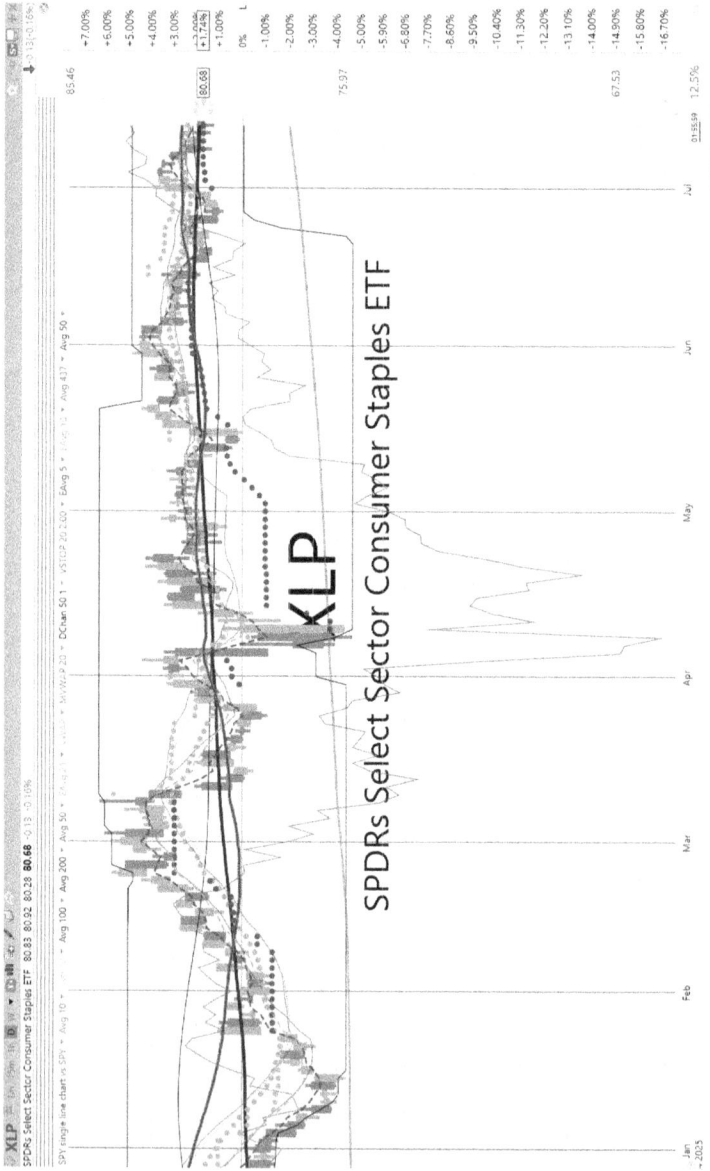

Chart provided by TC2000®

Figure 8. XLB (Materials)
+8.4740% YTD—Strong Buy Pattern

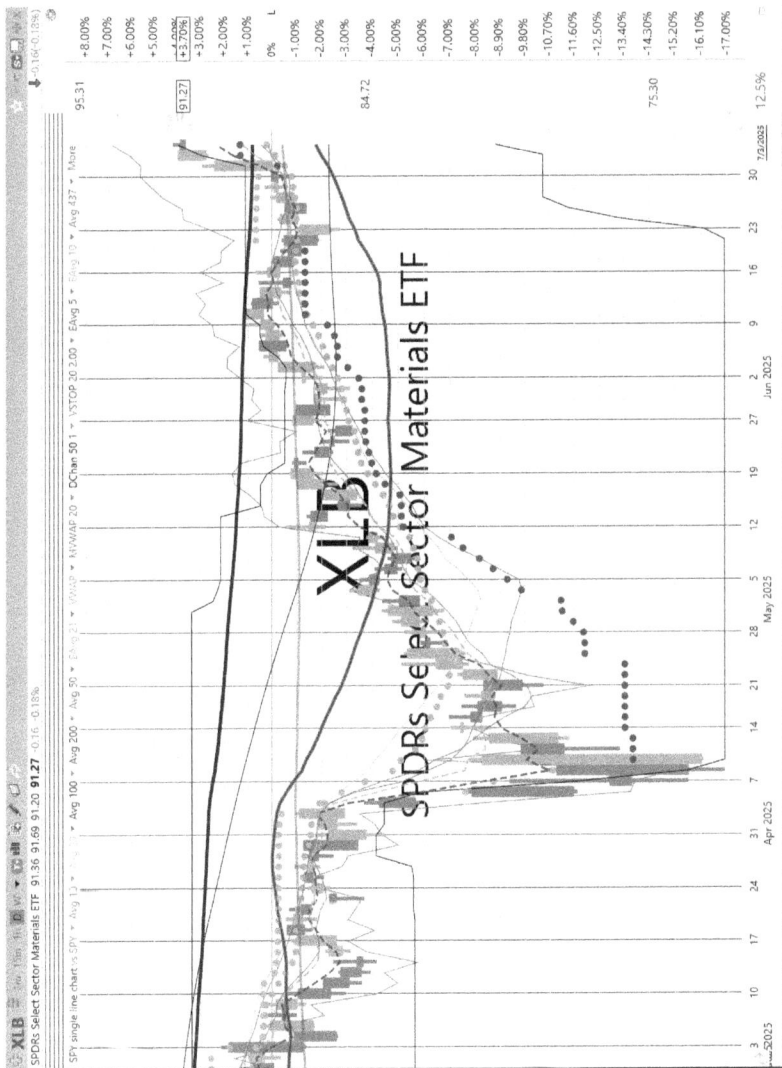

Chart provided by TC2000®

Figure 9. XLE (Energy)
+1.5953% YTD—Very Sloppy Sideways Pattern, No Buy

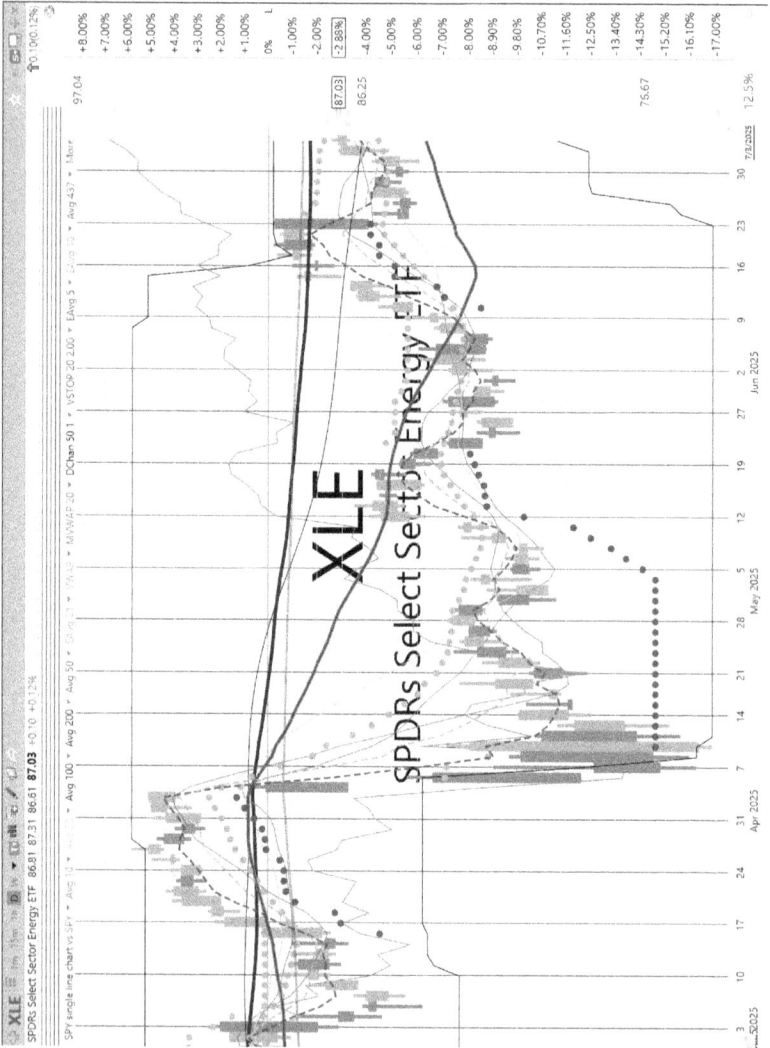

Chart provided by TC2000®

Figure 10. XLI (Industrials)
+13.3199% YTD—Very Strong Buy Pattern

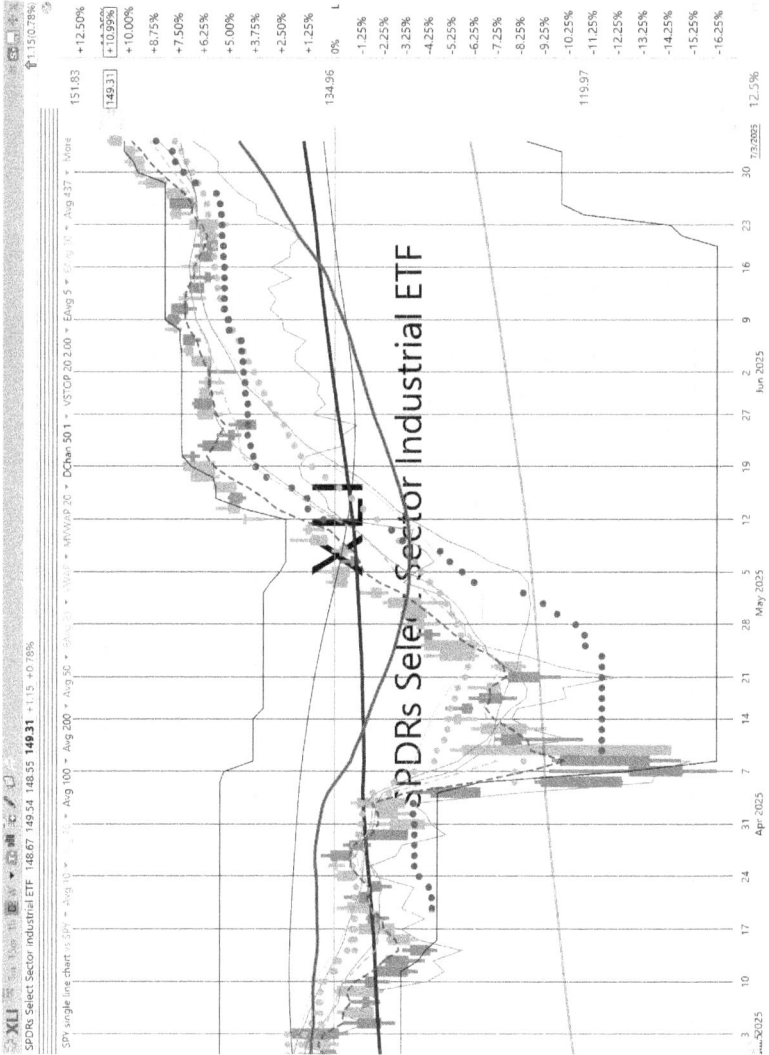

Chart provided by TC2000®

Figure 11. XLK (Information Technology)
+10.5152% YTD—Very Strong Buy Pattern

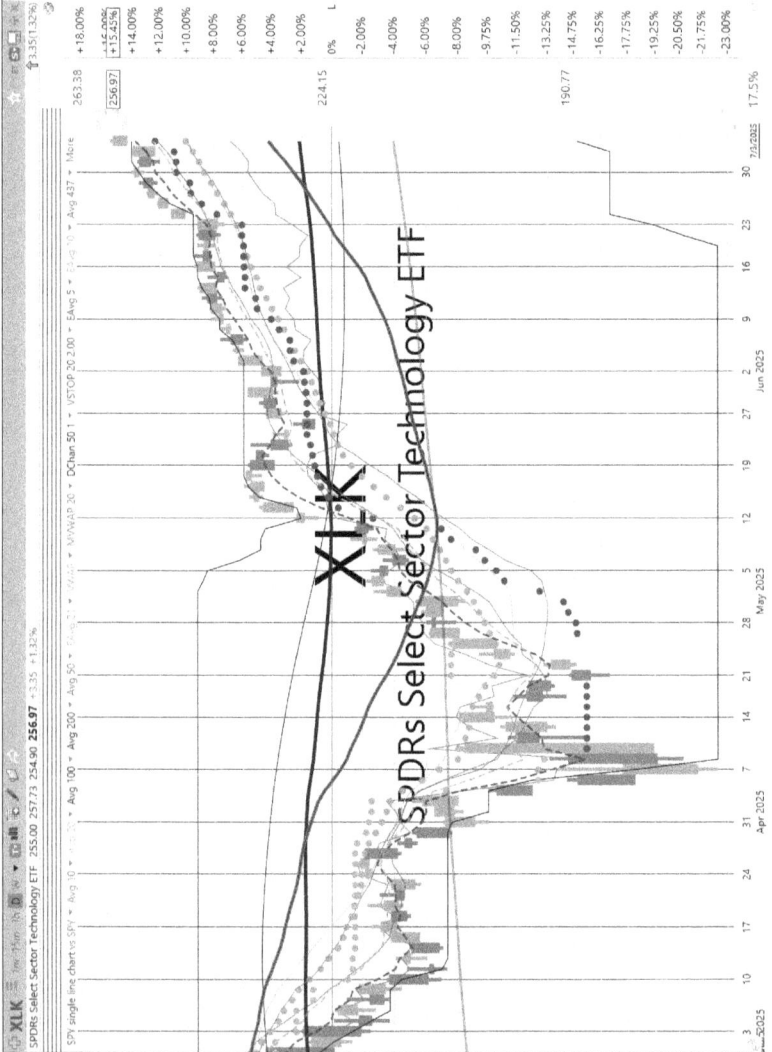

Chart provided by TC2000®

Figure 12. XLU (Utilities)
+7.9664% YTD—Weak Buy Pattern

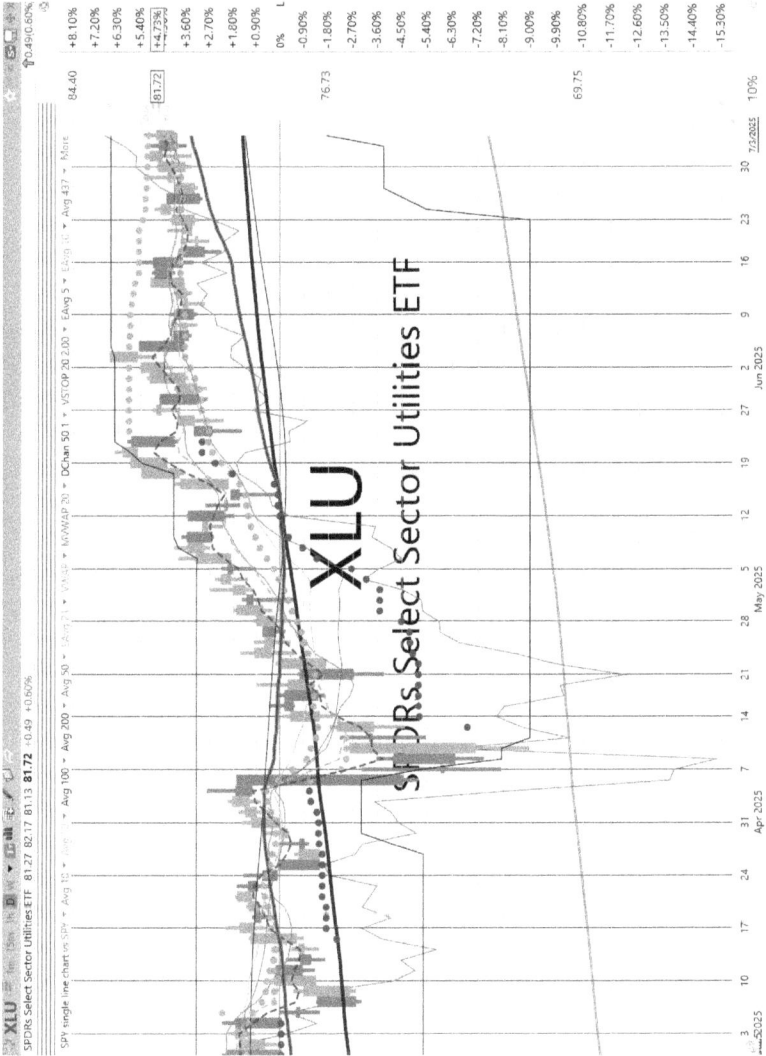

Chart provided by TC2000®

Figure 13. XLRE (Real Estate)

+2.8294% YTD—Sloppy Sideways Pattern, No Buy

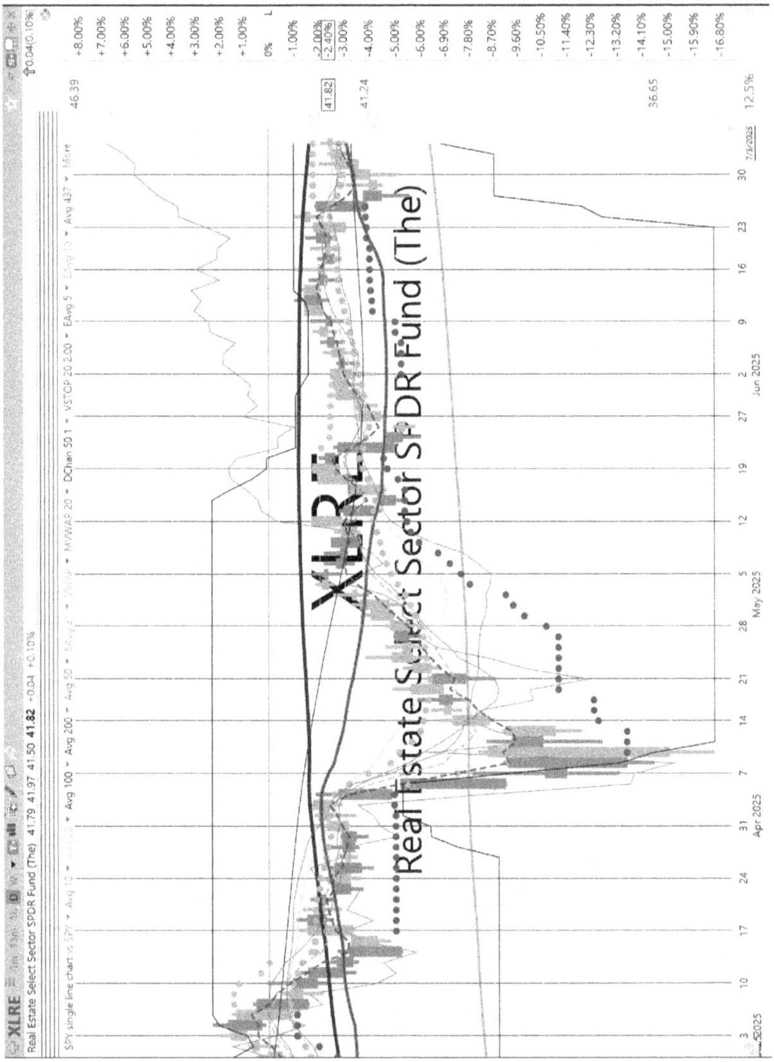

Chart provided by TC2000®

Figure 14. XLV (Healthcare)
-1.14538% YTD—Sell Pattern

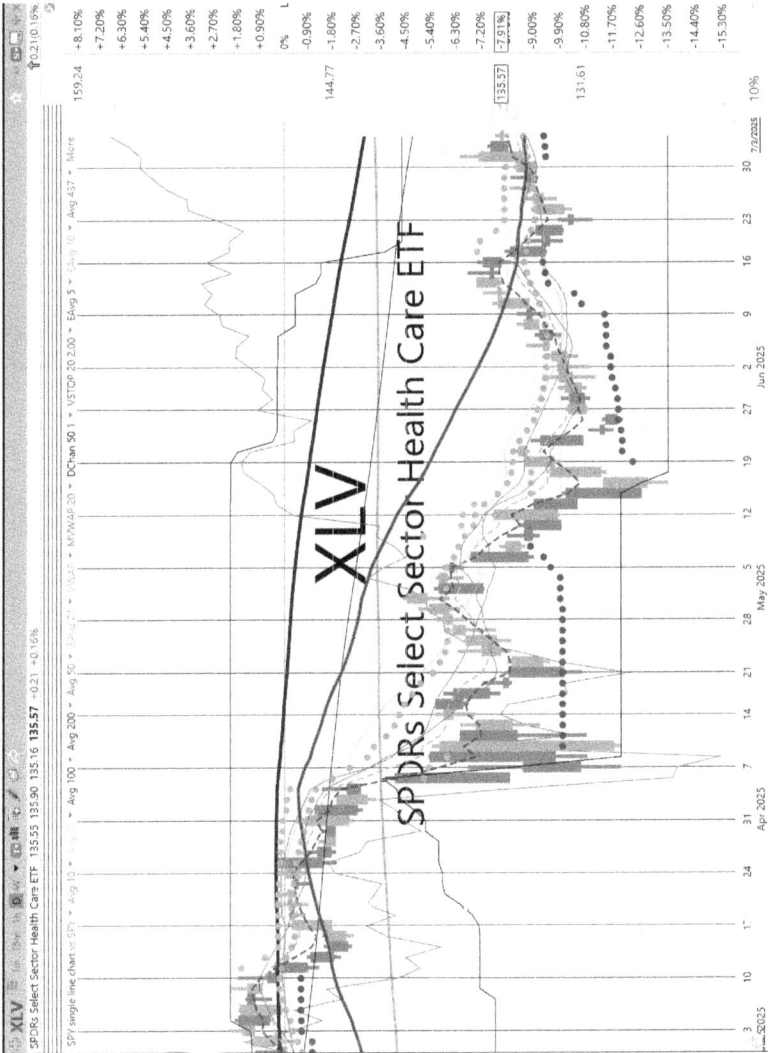

Chart provided by TC2000®

Figure 15. XLY (Consumer Discretionary)
-1.4932% YTD—Very Strong Buy Pattern

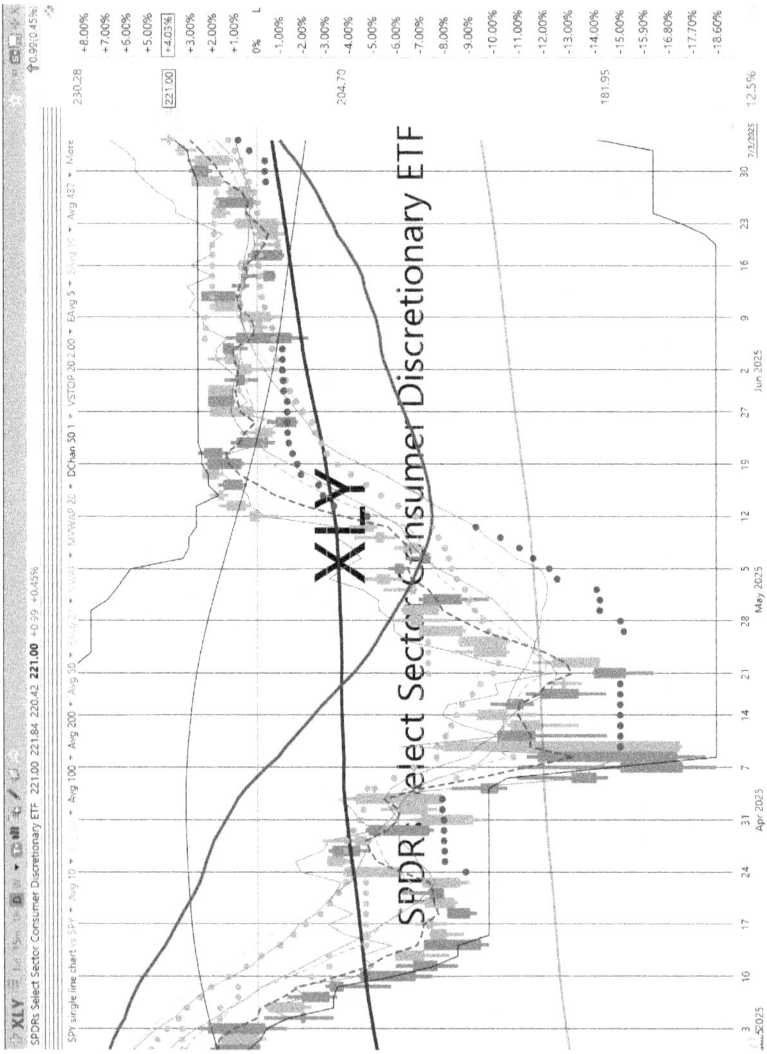

Chart provided by TC2000®

Examining the Eleven Charts and the MAGS

Clearly, the charts above show us to be in a solid bull market.

XLC, XLF, XLI, and XLK are the top four performers. XLP and XLU are positive for the year, but no one cares about them.

Even considering the Eleven Charts, the market is being driven by the MAGS chart below. The MAGS, the Magnificent Seven, represent a massive investment in technology (and by extension today, artificial intelligence companies), as you can tell by the business activity of each of the seven companies. They are involved in cloud computing, electric vehicle design and manufacture, and artificial intelligence. Not only are they all technology-based businesses, but they've historically outpaced the broader market, including our trusty S&P 500. Technology is thus recognized as a powerhouse in the market. When XLY is rising, consumers are spending. When XLF is rising, banks are lending. XLI is looking for the infrastructure spending to come down the pipeline.

As of 2025, these are the most commonly recognized MAGS stocks:

- Apple (AAPL)
- Microsoft (MSFT)
- Amazon (AMZN)
- Alphabet (GOOGL, Google's parent company)
- Meta Platforms (META, formerly Facebook)
- Nvidia (NVDA)
- Tesla (TSLA)

Figure 16. The Magnificent Seven (MAGS) Stocks

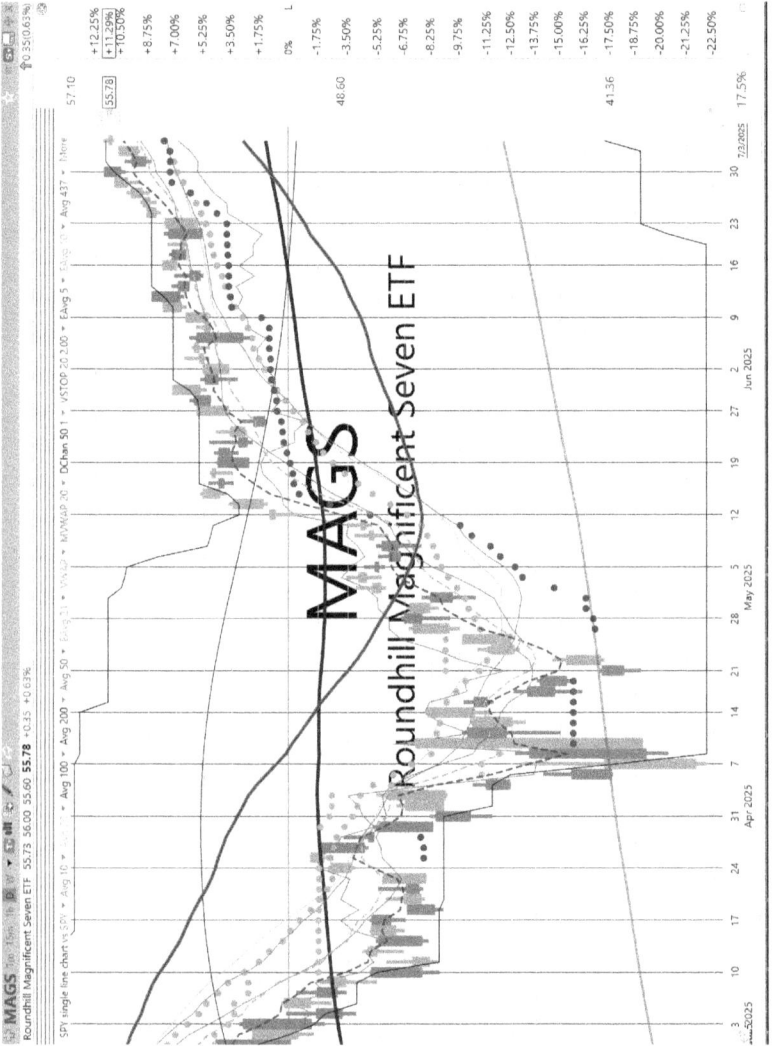

Chart provided by TC2000®

Consumer Discretionary Sector

Let me go back to XLY, the Consumer Discretionary sector, and show you why we watch it so closely.

You saw that the XLY chart showed it has lost value over the year-to-date (January to July 3, 2025, when I printed my chart). However, the chart has made a strong recovery since mid-February and continues to be a barometer for the consumer-spending crowd. *It shows they are no longer scared to spend money.*

Here are some top stocks in XLY, many of which you will recognize:

Airbnb	Lennar
Amazon	Lowe's
AutoZone	Marriott
Booking	McDonald's
Carnival	Nike
Chipotle	O'Reilly Automotive
DR Horton	PulteGroup
eBay	Ross Stores
Ford Motors	Royal Caribbean
Garmin	Starbucks
General Motors	Tesla
Hilton	TJX
Home Depot	Tractor Supply
Las Vegas Sands	Yum Brands

I provide them so you can see why XLY is an indicator that people who have "extra money" left at the end of the month are spending it. They travel, buy cars, eat out, improve property they own, and so on.

XLY needs to thrive for the country to have a thriving economy and a thriving stock market. Now, right now, XLY is on a screaming buy signal. If you go back to the week before the 2024 presidential election, you can see that XLY was in the toilet, shouting, "Sell me!"

I have to teach this to people. It's not about the S&P 500. We don't just look at the S&P 500 Page 4 Chart and wring our hands . . . or shout for joy. It's about which of those eleven sectors are the best or worst performing. Yes, the stocks in the Eleven Charts appear in the S&P 500, but for growth, you need to be able to compartmentalize and determine every day which ones are leading the pack of eleven.

That is how we make a data-driven buy or sell decision for our clients.

The other phenomenon is that bear markets tend to take down the big boy financial advisories because they are buy-and-hold pie chart promoters, right? One of the reasons my firm and our clients were +13 percent during the tech wreck is that we never did a buy-and-hold but rotated *out* of the sectors that were at risk, such as XLK (Technology), and *into* the high-performing (positive) ones.

In other words? There's another way of thinking about the stock market that your Pie Chart Promoter will never, ever talk to you about: the eleven-sector rotation strategy.

Style Boxes

There's another way of organizing the stock market. It's called the tic-tac-toe board, or the style boxes. You have three columns and three rows as shown below.

Table 8. Style Boxes

	Value	Blend	Growth
Large Cap	+12.51	+2.12	+0.82
Mid-Cap	+4.66	+2.16	-4.57
Small Cap	+6.61	+2.14	-1.88

Large-cap, mid-cap, and small-cap stocks are categories of market capitalization (the total number of outstanding shares multiplied by the current market price per share), not the share price itself. Here's how we define the categories of market capitalization:

- Large cap: $10 billion or more
- Mid-cap: $2 billion–$10 billion
- Small cap: $250 million–$2 billion

Quite often, when large-cap growth is getting the dirt kicked out of it, mid-cap and small-cap value are going up. The latter two go up when people won't buy large-cap growth because . . . it's getting the dirt kicked out of it. They go to a safe haven, which is quite often stocks of mid-cap and small-cap value.

While this is eighth-grade math as I present it here, the style boxes are more sophisticated in their usefulness for mixing and matching funds (our Eleven Charts) and analyzing the mix for portfolio diversification.[63] I won't get into the weeds of style boxes here, as that is not my purpose. I just want you to note that financial advisors (should) know this. They should be using this tool.

Keeping it simple, though, if I put a number in each of those nine boxes and say to a child, "Pick the best number," an eighth grader would go with the biggest number, and that's the one you buy.

It's a way to cross-check your methodology because you're coming at it from two different directions. You're seeking out the top three of the eleven sectors. And you have to understand why those three are in the top—are you seeing the bull (XLK, XLF, XLY) or the bear (XLU, XLP, XLE)?

I talk to salespeople in Home Depot and Lowe's. I talk to the waiters and waitresses in restaurants, and I ask them, "How's business? What's going on? Is business good? Is business slow?" When you have a bear market correction and the Michigan Consumer Confidence Index goes down, restaurant spending and discretionary spending go down.

In 2024, people weren't wandering into Home Depot on Saturday morning and dropping $100,000 on a new kitchen. That just wasn't happening. But right now, in 2025, it's happening. Even though interest rates are still high, people who have money are spending it (they are no longer scared).

Remember that today, 23 percent of the population has discretionary income, but 77 percent doesn't. And not only do they not have discretionary income, they also owe $1.21 trillion in credit card debt. Right now, people don't realize it, but the stock market is being kept alive by institutions that have money, such as hedge funds, but the retail investor is only 23 percent of investors. If you owe $1.21 trillion in credit card debt at 26 percent interest, you're not going to remodel your kitchen.

All you really need to do to see a bear versus bull market is ask people who work in Consumer Discretionary businesses how things are going. And depending upon the city you're in, it's boom or it's bust. Go to a car dealer in Sarasota, Florida, and you'll hear that they're selling a ton of cars. But in Baltimore, Maryland, they're not right now. It's regional.

When Biden was in office, interest rates were high and inflation was high, so the Magnificent Seven were getting seriously beat up. But after Inauguration Day, January 20, 2025, you can track the stock market going straight up. Then it pulled back a little because of inflation and consumer spending. Later, it rallied again.

None of this is an education you'll receive from any buy-and-hold Pie Chart Promoter. They simply don't like to talk about this, and their results don't prove that they know anything about it. My guess is that after reading this book, you'll know about their shenanigans and know more about how to protect your money than they do.

16
TEN BEST AND TEN
WORST DAYS

I want to present another way that Pie Chart Promoters practice misdirection on you. It's something I've been teaching people for twenty years. Buy-and-hold advisors use another market phenomenon to urge their clients to stay the course and feel the pain of the Bear.

I cited an article in chapter 4 that I want to bring back out for a different topic it addresses. It was called "2025 Teaches the Wisdom of Buy and Hold Investing"[64] from May 2025. The article was addressed specifically to advisors in ETF.com's "Advisor Section." Here's some of that "wisdom":

> According to a JPMorgan Asset Management study[65], an investor who remained fully invested in the S&P 500 for the past twenty years would

have seen a return of 10.6 percent annually. But if the investor missed just the ten best days over that twenty-year period, their return would drop to 6.4 percent. Missing the top twenty days? The return falls to 3.7 percent.

Keep the Ten Best and Avoid the Ten Worst

But what if you had a system that kept you from *ever* missing the gains of the ten best days but *always* helped you avoid the losses of the ten worst days? Or, put another way, what if you had a system to keep the best and avoid the worst?

The buy-and-hold advisors don't consider that a possibility, do they? They can't. It would crush their beloved buy-and-hold narrative.

But my firm does have such a strategy, and it has helped us beat the S&P. We've done it, and others like me have done it.

How? It starts with an analysis of moving averages.

Moving Averages

Moving averages are lines laid over the price chart. They work like this to give us information: If you're creating, say, a five-day average, you add up the closing prices of a stock for the last five days and divide by five.

What about the "moving" part? On Day 6, you subtract the price of Day 1 and add the price of Day 6, then divide the total by five. That's how to create a five-day *moving* average. And each day the process continues: Day 7 kicks out Day 2, Day 8 kicks out Day 3, and so on.

Of course, my team doesn't have to do all this crazy math in their heads. Our TC2000® system does it for us on any of thousands of stocks, ETFs, etc., that we choose. You've guessed that this is part of the technical analysis we do to benefit from the ten best and avoid the ten worst days. What do we do with a five-day moving average? We compare it with a ten-day moving average. Our TC2000® watches both numbers.

When Averages Cross

When prices start to rise, the moving averages naturally start to rise as well. When the five-day moving average crosses *up and over* the ten-day moving average, this is a "buy signal." And when the five-day moving average crosses *down and below* the ten-day moving average, we get a "sell signal."

Now, think about it. If we just watch and react to the five- and ten-day moving averages, we won't be able to keep *all* of the ten best days and avoid *all* of the ten worst days. In fact, in extremely volatile years, a "bear moving-average cross-down" often doubles as one of the ten worst-performing days. But reacting to a sell signal, which happens at the close of trading, does not enable you to avoid that day's losses.

To show you how moving average crosses can line up with the ten best- or ten worst-performing days, my team analyzed the S&P 500 during 2007. As you now know from prior chapters, 2007 was one of our most volatile years ever. My team found that using a moving-average trading strategy would enable you to capture the gains of four out of the ten best days. But you could avoid only one of the ten worst days using the moving-average strategy.

Let's look at some data.

2007's Ten Best-Performing Days

Table 8 below shows the best-performing days of the S&P 500 that year.

Table 8. S&P 500's Ten Best-Performing Days in 2007

Rank	Close	% Change	Bull MA-Cross Dates	Top 10 Bull Dates
9	1,416.60	+2.15	01-12	01-03
4	1,377.95	+2.37	02-01	03-13
10	1,435.04	+2.13	02-16	03-21
8	1,438.89	+2.20	03-12	04-11
7	1,511.04	+2.23	03-21	07-24
5	1,453.09	+2.35	04-05	08-09
2	1,411.27	+2.52	05-17	08-16
1	1,519.78	+2.92	06-01	09-18
3	1,554.41	+2.44	06-18	10-11
6	1,481.05	+2.31	08-30	11-13
			09-05	
			09-17	

Rank	Close	% Change	Bull MA-Cross Dates	Top 10 Bull Dates
			10-30	
			11-29	
			12-26	

In the fifth column, you see the ten best-performing days.

In the fourth column are the dates when the five-day moving average crossed up and over the ten-day moving average. This produces a buy signal. Here you can see that using a moving-average trading strategy, you can capture four of the top-ten days of gain, those shown in red in the fifth column.

2007's Ten Worst-Performing Days

In 2007, the moving-average trading strategy would enable you to avoid just one of the ten worst-performing days of the S&P 500 Index.

Table 9. S&P 500's Ten Worst-Performing Days in 2007

Rank	Close	% Change	Bear MA-Cross Dates	Top 10 Bear Dates
1	1,399.04	-3.48	02-27	02-27
7	1,377.95	-2.33	07-26	03-13
4	1,458.95	-2.66	08-03	07-26
5	1,433.06	-2.96	08-09	08-03
2	1,453.09	-2.35	08-28	08-09
9	1,406.70	-2.56	10-19	08-15

Rank	Close	% Change	Bear MA-Cross Dates	Top 10 Bear Dates
8	1,500.63	-2.65	11-01	10-19
6	1,508.44	-2.94	11-07	11-01
3	1,475.62	-2.33	11-26	11-07
10	1,439.18	-2.53	12-11	11-12

In the fifth column, I've listed the ten worst-performing days in 2007. In the fourth column are the dates when the five-day moving average crossed down and under the ten-day moving average. This produces a sell signal.

Here you can see that using a moving-average trading strategy, you could have avoided just one of the top-ten days of losses: 11-12. Selling on 11-07 would have prevented the losses of 11-12.

In this extremely volatile year, the moving-average cross days often produced a top-ten worst day as well (shown in blue in the table).

One Technique Does Not Make a Strategy

At my firm, we don't just use the moving-average strategy. As you've already guessed, that's just one strategy or tool in our kit. You've learned that we also use the eleven sector ETFs. We concentrate our holdings in XLK (Tech), XLF (Financial), and XLY (Consumer Discretionary) during bull markets. We move some of our clients' positions into XLU (Utilities), XLP (Consumer Staples), and XLE (Energy) during bear markets. This strategy accentuates the gains in a bull market and reduces losses in a bear market—which is the same as capturing the value of some of those best-forming days or avoiding the loss of some of those worst-performing days.

We have other methods, tools, strategies, and types of data in our analytical tool kit, but I promised: not too much technical stuff. Not only does our strategy protect our clients' wealth but it makes that wealth grow more and more. I'm sure you can understand by this point in your reading (and thanks to all you investing novices for reading this far) that not all money managers actively use these tools, tactics, and strategies on your behalf.

By using our total strategy, my team and I can often recoup any missed gains of the ten best days. We can often make up for losses suffered in the early days of the ten worst days.

So the bottom line is this: Yes, it is possible to keep most of the ten best days' gains and avoid most of the ten worst days' losses. You need a strategy, the information, and the tools. At RFS, we have it all.

Once again, the buy-and-hold advisors' clients are missing out. Don't be one of them! Far too many advisors ignore your best interests with their buy-and-hold, pie chart nonsense.

I'm sure you understand much better now what to look for and expect from a great financial advisor. Let me open your eyes to one more failure of many advisors.

17
THE TRUTH ABOUT
VARIABLE UNIVERSAL LIFE

Now, talking suddenly about life insurance may seem like I've left the subject at hand. Bear with me (pun intended), and you'll see that I'm still educating you. I'm still telling you about your financial (or, in this case, insurance) advisor. I'm still telling you what the advisor doesn't know or would rather just not tell you. I'm still telling you what I believe most of them are doing wrong.

There are two schools of thought about variable universal life (VUL) insurance.[66] Here they are: (1) It's terrible and (2) it's great.

Very funny, right, and not much help? I agree. The truth is that VUL insurance is neither. This split in opinions is due to dishonest salespeople willfully ignoring what and who VUL is designed for. Dishonest, yes, because it was specifically designed for affluent people.

Most people can't afford to buy Lamborghinis. Everyone gets that. Does that mean Lamborghinis are bad? Of course not. The answer is that rich people can afford them, and they're great cars for rich people to own. If a poor person tries to buy one, it's not going to end well.

VUL is the same way. Targeting the wrong buyers started years ago, and one company, Ameriprise, went too far. Do you know why American Express sold American Express Financial Services[67] and renamed it Ameriprise[68] back in 2006? I know this from people there, including the managing partner of the accounting firm involved in the transaction. The American Express legal team told them they were looking at hundreds of millions of dollars of liability lawsuits. Who would sue them? The people who were improperly sold VUL.[69] Internally, they realized they were wide open to lawsuits, and no company wants that.

Who *should* buy VUL? Rich people. First, no salesperson should sell it to people who have less than $3 million, *and* a sustainable income, *and* an earnings outlook of over $400,000/year, *and* average or better health. *And* they should not be over fifty years of age. Second, VUL needs a minimum of twenty years of accumulation to make the performance work. It is not a last-minute investment.

These are my guidelines, not written rules or regulations.

Salespeople, though? They do sell to clients with lesser wealth and health (alas for their reputations).

On the other hand, you hear VUL is great because it's the biggest tax shelter left to us, and this is true if you meet the guidelines above. You put in after-tax non-qualified dollars, and all the growth comes out 100 percent state and federal income-tax-free. It's also estate-tax-free. It's free of all taxes if you follow the rules. One rule relates to the modified endowment contract (MEC), which I won't discuss, but your advisor needs to mention it. You have to understand it too.[70] It's possible to make life insurance taxable, but the examples are rare. What I want you to know are the two most common ways to keep your life insurance 100 percent estate-tax-free:

1. A competent insurance professional will make sure the beneficiary *is also the owner*, which guarantees the death proceeds are estate-tax-free. Many life insurance owners don't know that "owner" is part of the contract; they just think of the "insured" and the "beneficiary."

2. Married couples, particularly with children, *also* need a full set of comprehensive estate planning documents, and a popular strategy is the irrevocable life insurance trust (ILIT). When the owner and beneficiary are both the ILIT, you have estate-tax-free death benefit proceeds, and the ILIT should have a tax ID number and a checking account designated for paying the life insurance premiums.

I wish I could tell you the following has never happened, but I see it several times a year: A client or relative passes. I get the phone call. We all get together and meet. Someone brings in the very expensive leatherbound binder of estate planning documents, and they're all blank and never signed. Or they are signed, but none of the documents have been funded. "Not funded" means the life insurance policies are not in the ILITs, as the change of owner and beneficiary paperwork has never been completed.

Please have your estate planning documents completed, signed, and funded. The cost range of this process, depending on where you live, can be anywhere from $3,000 to $8,000, sometimes more. Make sure you have done and followed *all* your attorney's instructions. I am sorry to say that incomplete or unfunded trusts are a very common oversight that lets the tax man barge through your door.

VUL is, without question, the premier, number one tax shelter on the planet for affluent people. If you meet the guidelines I gave for it, sit down with a CPA or a tax attorney who advises affluent people. They'll tell you, "If you can pass the insurance physical, you want to buy the biggest VUL policies you can afford. They're tax shelters." That means the VUL is for those who can sock between $300,000 and $1 million into the policy over seven to ten years. It's not for middle managers or union workers making $80,000 per year or with a net worth of $250,000.

A High-Return True Story

I want to share a true story with you. In 1992, I purchased an insurance agency from a very good friend, who was one of my instructors for the Chartered Life Underwriter® certification in 1974. He's a very bright and very well-connected individual, a Wharton grad as well. He was bored with insurance and was starting a telecom resale business with friends.

Now, here I'll interrupt myself mid-story. For the story to make sense, I have to get a bit into the weeds of licensing. The good news about this opportunity is that my friend, the seller, didn't have a FINRA series 6 or 7 insurance license.[71] This fellow had only state life and health licenses. As such, his entire book was life insurance contracts and fixed annuities, all general account contracts, with no investment upside.

In all humility, I devoured it like a pride of hungry lions. Every client who could afford it and pass a physical got the Nationwide Life "Best of America IV" VUL contract, which was absolutely one of the five best in the business at the time. We did the same thing with the fixed annuity contracts. They all went to the same Nationwide Life "Best of America" variable annuity (VA) contract.

I would like to clarify here the advantages of this type of contract. Both the life and the annuity versions have an investment menu of 140-plus options. When we apply the technical analysis trading strategies from the earlier chapters of the book, the client pays *no* commissions, *no* transfer fees, and *no* taxes of any type.

We proceeded to knock the ball out of the park with gains as high as 655 percent over fourteen-plus years (see the performance table in figure 18, under Total Period for Graph 1). The green line in figure 18 shows our firm's portfolio growth over the chart's 1994–2007 time frame.[72]

Figure 17. Keystone Capital Management
Clients vs. Major Indexes

Keystone Capital Management, Inc.

Thursday February 8 2007 2:02 PM
Rpt# 95824   Page 1 of 1

MOUNTAIN CHARTS
(Percent & Transaction Flows)

Graph 1 ——— Client--401001 - LBL+(Gross#1-)
Graph 2 ——— Z#0000 --Buy/Hold+S&P500(TotalReturn)+(Gross)
Graph 3 ——— Z#0000 --Buy/Hold+NASDAQCompositeIndex+(Gross)
Graph 4 ——— Z#0000 --Buy/Hold+DJIndustrialAverageIndex+(Gross)

07/05/1994 to 01/23/2007

	PERFORMANCE											
	RETURN					**RISK (Measures)**				**RISK (Maximum Drawdown)**			
Graph	Total Period	Compnd Annual	Risk Adjusted Alpha	Sharpe	UPI	Corr. r^2	Beta	Ann'lzd St Dev	Ulcer Index	Peak Date	Bottom Date	End Date	Max. Loss	Max. Mos
Graph 1	655.0%	17.5%	11.9%	1.38	3.91	0.19	0.25	10.1%	-3.7%	03/10/00	04/14/00	09/01/00	-12.0%	23.3
Graph 2	295.6%	11.6%	0.0%	0.44	.49	1.00	1.00	18.3%	-17.0%	09/01/00	10/09/02	10/25/06	-47.5%	73.3
Graph 3	245.6%	10.4%	-3.8%	0.22	.16	0.71	1.32	30.4%	-43.9%	03/10/00	10/09/02	OPEN	-77.9%	82.5
Graph 4	243.2%	10.3%	-0.6%	0.38	.61	0.88	0.92	18.0%	-11.7%	01/14/00	10/09/02	10/03/06	-37.8%	80.6

Note 1: Bold typeface indicates the "winner."
Note 2: Periodic Rebalance -- None (Strict separate streams.)

Total Deposits.....	$846,419
Total Withdrawals	-$500,005
Net Investment...	$346,414
Total Management Fees.	-$286,309
Account Gain/Loss.......	$4,703,061
Current Market Value.....	$4,431,618

Well, back to my friend who sold me the business. He called me up two years later, in early 1994. He said, "I've been hearing really great things from my former clients about you and your success with variable universal life and variable annuities. Can you help me with my mom?"

I replied with the normal, "Is your mom in good health? Can she pass an insurance physical?"

"Absolutely," he replied.

He sent me all the documents and the contract, as this policy was not part of the agency purchase. Long story short, his mom owned a $2.5 million whole-life policy with New York Life Insurance Company. It had a cash value of $846,419. She passed the physical, and we did an IRS section 1035 exchange[73] of the cash value to her new VUL contract, with an approved face value of the same $2.5 million.

A few years after that, my friend needed $500,000 to buy into an advertising agency as a part owner. He took a tax-free loan from the policy, leaving the contract with a basis of $346,419 (his mom's original $846,419 minus his $500,000 loan). When his mom passed away in early 2008, the account value was $4,703,063, and the death benefit was over $5.1 million.

In short, I took his mother's policy with its cash value of $346,419 and turned it into $5.1 million in thirteen and a half years. That's a gain of 1,372 percent from July 5, 1994, to January 23, 2007. Do more math, and it gives us a very admirable CAGR (compound annual growth rate) of over

22 percent per year. May I remind you that the S&P 500 and the AGG are far—so far—from offering that kind of annual return?

You might say, "Whoa, Jack! No way. Who does that?! What the . . .?"

Yes, my math is good. Yes, you're reading the correct numbers. This was in spite of Mom's son, my friend, having drawn down $500,000 as a tax-free loan.

And, to be very, very clear: This was not a one-off! Of course, such results are subject to their starting dates, deposits, and withdrawals—as you know from our discussion of the S&P 500 as a big swimming pool—which all have an impact on investment performance.

The $5.1 million was 100 percent state, county, city, and federal income and estate *tax-free*. That was because we knew the rules and followed them to the letter.

I must repeat something that's important but that American Express Financial Services got wrong back in the day. It's that aspect of this investment that so many advisors ignore: It's not for everyone. You need to talk with an advisor who understands your financial picture, the MEC, and the Technical and Miscellaneous Revenue Act (TAMRA) rules for life insurance. We will send you to an estate attorney to create an ILIT and tell you the truth.

So now you know the truth about the VUL. It's a financial Lamborghini for affluent investors.

THE CLOSING BELL

A lot of Americans have short memories when it comes to stock market booms and crashes. We forget the consequences we suffered because of them.

Those official bear markets of more than -20 percent are a reality. The havoc that an unofficial but still-painful decline can wreak in your life is real.

We've seen official bears twenty-two times in the last ninety-nine years, with an average decline of 38 percent. The bears will come back around to challenge us every four and a half years on average.

I will never believe anyone who says they're mentally prepared to lose 40 percent or more of their capital. Denial that another bear market will sooner or later occur is not the answer. A competent advisor's job is to keep your money safe. Their job is to stop you from making bad, emotional, panic-driven decisions.

Questions to Ask a Potential Advisor

You need to ask your current investment advisor some tough questions. They may make you both uncomfortable. I gave you the two primary interview questions for any advisor you're considering:

1. During the bear markets shown on this Page 4 Chart, what strategy or steps did you take to protect your clients' money?
2. Can you give me the names of three clients who will speak to me about your services?

As you now know, many advisors will implode rather than answer you. As you now realize, their buy-and-hold strategy only works (if it ever did) in a bull market.

During your interviews, also get the answer to this question:

3. Were you in the financial advisory business in 2008?

Were they in business for the dot-com bubble burst of 2000–02 or the Great Recession of 2007–09? I bring this up because over half of advisors have less than ten years' experience. In 2025, this means they began in 2015 or later. If your advisor has been in business for over ten years, ask this next question:

4. Between October 10, 2007, and March 6, 2009, how much of your clients' money did you lose?

Don't back down; demand an answer. They may answer. They'll more likely hem and haw. They may just turn purple. Chances are good that they'll silently escort you out of their offices. The latter is its own answer, isn't it?

Questions to Ask Yourself

You should likewise ask yourself some basic questions to identify where you are in your relationship with money.

1) What is the maximum loss of money I can tolerate at this point in my life?

This question alone causes a lot of anxious reflection. Some investors never register one very painful fact: Whatever percentage they say they're willing to risk might just represent several years' earnings for them. Is that 30 percent loss you say is "Fine, just fine," actually four years of take-home pay?

2) What is my advisor's current strategy to mitigate investment losses?

Did your advisor explain it—or blow you off? If you got no explanation, you moved on, right? You found a new advisor, right? You know about the Eleven Charts. Does your advisor?

3) Is my portfolio as diversified as my advisor would have me believe?

Or . . . have they stuck your money in several mutual funds with a lot of crossovers that don't earn you any real money? You are moving your money out of those funds, aren't you?

4) Is my portfolio 60/40 or some other pie chart allocation?

Did your advisor assign you to a pie chart, and if so, why that one? Is it actually based on your risk tolerance? Have you considered you're with the wrong advisor or brokerage firm? You should know the answer by now.

5) Is my advisor actually a fiduciary or only a Pie Chart Promoter?

Is your advisor doing buy-and-hold, only giving your account lip service? Are they really a Certified Financial Planner® (CFP®)? Look no further: If they're an employee of a big brokerage firm, guess what? They work for the firm, not for you.

Real advisors are fee-based. They don't earn commissions above and beyond those fees. They are affiliated with a major custodian, such as Charles Schwab.

Read your contract with your financial advisor. You might be alarmed to find out they're a broker and not a CFP® or subject to the fiduciary rules of taking care of the client first and acting in the client's best interests.

Read every word on their website. If you see even a hint that *you* need to align with *their* investment strategy? Run! If you see even a hint of "We're positive and we're holding on through this bear market"? Grab your money and run *fast*. Also, if they're selling you proprietary mutual funds, then your purchase most likely benefits their house much more than yours.

If you're a young investor, meaning you have twenty or more years left to work and save, start interviewing real fiduciaries today. You need real money managers who use technical analysis and a buy-sell strategy. You need advisors who know how to move your money from one sector to another (the Eleven Charts) to protect it in plenty of time, and grow it into the greater wealth you expect and have worked so hard to create.

If I've taught you nothing else by this point, you surely know that buy-and-hold is not an investment strategy. It's not the best option in a rising bull market, and it's devastating in a declining bear market. It's a set-it-and-forget-it method of giving a lazy advisor a way out of actually managing your money. Multiple mutual funds are also a lazy advisor's way of being paid for not doing the job.

I hope your chosen advisor proactively books meetings with you and takes any meetings you request. Insist on having a sit-down with your advisor twice a year and anytime you have financial or life changes to accommodate. Don't be afraid to talk about *your* money and how it's being protected and grown as much as possible. Regularly review your needs, goals, and risk tolerance. Have this conversation with the person who is supposed to be looking out for you.

It's amazing that so many investors own luxury autos with a hundred safety features integrated into them right at purchase: anti-lock brakes, airbags, lane change motion sensors, and so on. Yet their portfolio has no safety features built in.

I like to open our chart analysis software with clients. I show them how we use a few of our technical indicators to identify exit and entry points. I explain how the right exit/entry serves to protect and increase their wealth.

At RFS, we didn't get clobbered by those five bear markets, meaning our clients didn't lose their shirts—and we can prove it. We don't hide our methods or results.[74] Quite the contrary. As I discussed when we talked about the ten best and ten worst days, our clients were poised to *continue* making gains rather than having to first play catch-up.

I think I've shown you that not all financial advisors are created equal. Identify and work with one who is a true fiduciary—taking your goals, needs, and prosperity to heart.

What I Believe

I believe that every financial advisor worth their salt needs to be transparent with clients.

The market might look like a "win some, lose some" board game until you know the whole truth. We would all like it to be a "win some, and win some more" proposition as much as it can be. Far too many advisors don't even come close.

I do hope investing novices will read this book. I believe I'm a teacher, and I never assume a prospective client knows anything about the stock markets. After all, isn't that why they came to talk with us in the first place—for our knowledge, for our expert management? As I've said elsewhere in these pages, I educate them a little bit—as I hope I've done for you.

You know more now even though the industry stays silent. It neatly avoids giving you the information and the management you need. I, however, have been singing to you. I saw it as my duty to warn you of investment and advisor red flags. I've given you a peek at how a truly great advisor with your best interests at heart will work behind the scenes to first protect and then also wisely grow your wealth.

Save what you can, definitely. If it's $30,000 per year, $1,000 per month, or $50 per paycheck, save. If you're starting to contribute to 401(k) plans, or somehow saving the maximum you can, do that. Then get with the right advisor to keep that money safe and grow it into wealth.

Don't lose your shirt to the bears. Don't give your hard-earned, wisely saved money to the wrong advisor.

I hope by now you know *not* to make the mistake of parking your hard-saved money in some losing pie chart. You know now: There is a strategy and system for caging the bears. There is a way to maximize your investment returns. You know better now.

You can sleep peacefully every night . . . even when those Pie Chart Promoters and those television talking heads shout, "Well, folks, it's down another 15 percent. But it always bounces back!"

I hope I've educated you about bear markets and how to detect them. I hope you see that there have been five official bear markets since 1997 and know the risks of the numerous unofficial declines. You now realize you no longer have to be mauled and eaten alive by the next bears that come along.

I have over nine hundred clients. If you would like some references from me, get in touch and just ask. I can give you the names of clients who have already agreed to talk with you: doctors, lawyers, accountants, schoolteachers, first responders, business executives, federal government PhDs, airplane pilots, retired military members, and so on.

My team and I deploy strategies to protect and grow wealth. Our strategies cage all those bears, so ask me how we can do the same for you.

ABOUT THE AUTHOR

John (Jack) Reutemann Jr. has spent fifty-two years in the financial services industry. He has been featured as a keynote speaker at dozens of industry conferences. Jack teaches regularly throughout the country, where he guides financial professionals in using innovative strategies and processes.

Jack is not only the founder and CEO of Research Financial Strategies but also an advocate of modern investment strategies and a resource whom clients and other financial advisors seek for advice.

With fifty-two years of experience as an investment advisor representative, Jack has spent the last thirty years developing Research Financial Strategies into a multi-state registered investment advisor firm. The firm has offices in Maryland, Virginia, Ohio, Georgia, Tennessee, and California. Its clients hail from forty-seven US states, Europe, and Asia.

The firm is proud of its investing strategy that helped to avoid declines in prior stock market corrections. Research Financial Strategies specializes in providing investment advice using a proprietary methodology that leverages technical analysis.

Jack has been a frequent guest and expert contributor to CNBC, Fox News, and other national media outlets. As co-founder and co-instructor of No More Pies, he helps educate financial advisors on technical analysis and risk management. He's also a staunch advocate for the use of exchange-traded funds (ETFs) as a lower-cost and more efficient substitute for mutual funds.

Jack is a native Washingtonian. He attended St. John's Military High School and earned his bachelor's degree in economics and finance from the University of Maryland. He takes an active role in his community by supporting many charitable causes.

Jack and his wife Toni are residents of Sarasota, Florida, and spend seven months there and five months in Potomac, Maryland, every year visiting family and friends.

They've raised five children and are currently spoiling their nine grandchildren.

Learn more about Research Financial Strategies at RFSAdvisors.com.

ENDNOTES

Note to readers: I wrote this book throughout the summer of 2025. The Page 4 Chart I have referenced goes only to the end of June 2025, so keep that in mind as you read.

All the online sources I reference in hyperlinks and/or in the following endnotes were accessible as of July 31, 2025. Please note that the owners of those sources may have deleted or modified them by the time you read my book.

The Opening Bell

1   Ward Williams, "Timeline of Recorded Stock
    Market Crashes," Investopedia, October
    30, 2024, https://www.investopedia.com/
    timeline-of-stock-market-crashes-5217820.
2   "10/19/87 | CBS Evening News - Black Monday,"
    posted August 15, 2019, by Rochester TV Archive,
    YouTube, 29 min., 59 sec., https://www.youtube.com/
    watch?v=76DbHi8e9Ws

3   CBS News, "From the Archives: 'Black Monday,' the 1987 Stock Market Crash," original broadcast October 19, 1987, posted October 19, 2022, on YouTube, 53 sec., https://www.youtube.com/watch?v=cOuRwMW-Mrc.

4   Williams, "Timeline of Recorded Stock Market Crashes."

5   Brian Baker, "Biggest Stock Market Crashes in US History," Bankrate, April 3, 2025, https://www.bankrate.com/investing/biggest-stock-market-crashes-in-us-history.

6   Williams, "Timeline of Recorded Stock Market Crashes."

7   Jesse Pound, "U.S. Stock Market Loses $5 Trillion in Value in Three Weeks," CNBC, March 14, 2025, https://www.cnbc.com/2025/03/14/us-stock-market-loses-5-trillion-in-value-in-three-weeks.html.

8   Joseph Adinolfi, "U.S. Stocks See Biggest 2-Day Wipeout in History as Market Loses $11 Trillion Since Inauguration Day," MarketWatch, April 4, 2025, https://www.marketwatch.com/story/u-s-stocks-poised-for-biggest-two-day-wipeout-in-history-as-marketloses-9-6-trillion-since-inauguration-day-430919f6.

9   Peter Cohan, "Stocks Lose $9.6 Trillion — Here's How to Limit the Plunge's Pain," *Forbes*, April 8, 2025, https://www.forbes.com/sites/petercohan/2025/04/06/stocks-lose-96-trillion---how-to-limit-the-next-plunges-pain.

PART ONE: THOSE KILLER BEARS
Chapter 1: Bears Are Killers. So Are Bear Markets.

10   Saqib Iqbal Ahmed, "S&P 500 Correction in Six Charts," Reuters, March 15, 2025, https://www.reuters.com/markets/wealth/sp-500-correction-six-charts-2025-03-13.

11   James Carville, "James Carville and Mike Murphy Discuss the Fallout from the 2024 Election and Trump's Second Term," PBS, January 21, 2025, https://www.pbs.org/video/james-carville-and-mike-murphy-w4kwdk.

12   Shu-Sen Chang, David Stuckler, Paul Yip, and David Gunnell, "Impact of 2008 Global Economic Crisis on Suicide: Time Trend Study in 54 Countries," *BMJ* 347 (2013): f5239, https://www.bmj.com/content/347/bmj.f5239.

13   Melanie Haiken, "More Than 10,000 Suicides Tied to Economic Crisis, Study Says," *Forbes*, June 12, 2014, https://www.forbes.com/sites/melaniehaiken/2014/06/12/more-than-10000-suicides-tied-to-economic-crisis-study-says.

14   James Gallagher, "Recession 'Led to 10,000 Suicides,'" BBC, June 12, 2014, https://www.bbc.com/news/health-27796628.

Chapter 2: Those Killer Bears

15 This is a collation of statistics from annual reports. RealtyTrac® is an organization that provides foreclosure homes and properties for buyers and investors, so it updates data regularly for its own purposes. See *2008 U.S. Foreclosure Market Report* (RealtyTrac, 2009), posted on Yumpu, September 20, 2015, https://www.yumpu.com/en/ document/view/54019836/pdf-2008-foreclosure-market- report-from-realtytrac; "RealtyTrac® Year-End Report Shows Record 2.8 Million U.S. Properties with Foreclosure Filings in 2009 – an Increase of 21 Percent from 2008 and 120 Percent from 2007," press release, RealtyTrac, January 14, 2010, posted on Financial Crisis Inquiry Commission, Stanford University, https://fcic-static.law.stanford.edu/ cdn_media/fcic-docs/2010-01-14%20RealtyTrac%20 Year-End%20Report%20Shows%20Record%20 2.8%20Million%20US%20Properties%20with%20 Foreclosure%20Filing.pdf; and Rakesh Kochhar, Ana Gonzalez-Barrera, and Daniel Dockterman, *Through Boom and Bust: Minorities, Immigrants and Homeownership* (Pew Research Center, 2009), https://www.pewresearch.org/ race-and-ethnicity/2009/05/12/through-boom-and-bust.

16 Jason N. Houle and Michael T. Light, "The Home Foreclosure Crisis and Rising Suicide Rates, 2005 to 2010," *American Journal of Public Health* 104, no. 6 (June 2014): 1073–79, https://doi.org/10.2105/AJPH.2013.301774.

17   FRED, graph of corporate equities and mutual fund shares ownership by wealth percentile, July 10, 1988, to January 1, 2025, Board of Governors of the Federal Reserve System, https://fred.stlouisfed.org/graph/?g=Y8rM.

18   Yoel Minkoff, "Deeper Dive: The Wealthiest 10% of Americans Own 90% of the Stock Market," Seeking Alpha, July 2, 2025, https://seekingalpha.com/news/4464647-deeper-dive-the-wealthiest-10-of-americans-own-90-of-the-stock-market.

19   "The Impacts of Individual and Household Debt on Health and Well-Being," American Public Health Association, October 25, 2021, https://www.apha.org/policy-and-advocacy/public-health-policy-briefs/policy-database/2022/01/07/the-impacts-of-individual-and-household-debt-on-health-and-well-being.

20   Matt Schulz, "2025 Credit Card Debt Statistics," LendingTree, August 6, 2025, https://www.lendingtree.com/credit-cards/study/credit-card-debt-statistics.

21   Matt Bruenig, "How Many People Live Paycheck to Paycheck?," People's Policy Project, March 19, 2025, https://www.peoplespolicyproject.org/2025/03/19/how-many-people-live-paycheck-to-paycheck.

22   Keshav Srikant, "Fact Check: Is There a Consensus That a Majority of Americans Are Living Paycheck to Paycheck?," EconoFact, February 26, 2025, https://econofact.org/fact-brief/is-there-a-consensus-that-a-majority-of-americans-are-living-paycheck-to-paycheck.

23   Melissa Repko, "Home Depot May Need an Interest Rate
     Cut to Boost Its Sales," CNBC, August 13, 2024, https://
     www.cnbc.com/2024/08/13/home-depot-q2-earnings-fed-
     interest-rate-cut-may-boost-sales.html.

24   Greg Daugherty, "Here's How Much Americans Save
     for Retirement: How Do You Compare?," Investopedia,
     December 13, 2024, https://www.investopedia.com/
     average-retirement-savings-by-age-8740967.

Chapter 3: The Buy-and-Hold Insanity

25   Daniel Liberto, "This Is the Single Best Investing
     Move You Can Make in 2025," Investopedia,
     January 24, 2025, https://www.investopedia.com/
     single-best-investing-move-8778947.

26   Kent Thune, "2025 Teaches the Wisdom of Buy
     and Hold Investing," ETF.com, May 15, 2025,
     https://www.etf.com/sections/advisor-center/
     buy-and-hold-strategy-market-timing-2025.

PART TWO: WHEN THE BEAR EATS YOU
Chapter 4: The Current Narrative

27   Dan Kemp, "Morningstar's 2025 Investment Outlook
     for Financial Advisors," Morningstar, November 22,
     2024, https://www.morningstar.com/financial-advisors/
     morningstars-2025-investment-outlook-financial-advisors.

28   Francis M. Kinniry Jr., "Market Volatility Is Inevita-
     ble—Advisor's Alpha® Is Enduring," Vanguard, March
     31, 2025, https://advisors.vanguard.com/insights/article/
     market-volatility-is-inevitable-advisors-alpha-is-enduring.

29   "The Climb Back: What Past Downturns Tell Us About
      the Road to Recovery," Merrill Lynch, accessed September
      2, 2025, https://www.ml.com/articles/managing-market-
      downturns-volatility.html.

30   Anthony Saglimbene, "Despite How It Feels, We've
      Been Here Before," posted May 14, 2025, by Ameriprise
      Financial, Facebook, 2 min., 35 sec., https://www.facebook.
      com/watch/?v=1877895836363786.

31   Ron Wyden, "Wyden Rips into Trump Trade Rep Over
      Tariffs: Our Economy Is a Laughingstock," posted April
      8, 2025, by Ron Wyden, YouTube, 5 min., 33 sec., https://
      www.youtube.com/watch?v=1ti2Efm914g.

32   The SEC was created in the aftermath of the Wall Street
      crash of 1929 with a primary mission of enforcing laws
      against market manipulation.

33   *2008 Year in Review and Annual Financial Report: Reform-
      ing Regulation to Better Protect Investors* (Financial Industry
      Regulatory Authority, 2009), https://www.finra.org/about/
      annual-reports/archive.

34   Richard G. Ketchum, *2009 FINRA Year in Review* (Finan-
      cial Industry Regulatory Authority, 2010). https://www.
      finra.org/about/annual-reports/archive.

35   Bob Clark, "Are RIAs Really a Bigger Regulatory
      Problem Than Brokers?," ThinkAdvisor, March 20,
      2012, https://www.thinkadvisor.com/2012/03/20/
      are-rias-really-a-bigger-regulatory-problem-than-brokers.

36   "Dump FINRA and the SEC," *Forbes*, September 10, 2009,
      https://www.forbes.com/2009/09/10/regulation-finra-sec-
      intelligent-investing-fines.html.

Chapter 5: Buy-and-Hold Should Be a Crime

37   Stephanie Horan, "How Are Financial Advisors and
      Investors Responding to the Bear Market? – 2022 Study,"
      SmartAsset, August 9, 2025, https://smartasset.com/
      data-studies/how-are-financial-advisors-and-investors-
      responding-to-the-bear-market-2022.

38   "Final Rule: Investment Adviser Codes of Ethics,"
      US Securities and Exchange Commission, July 9,
      2004, https://www.sec.gov/rules-regulations/2004/07/
      investment-adviser-codes-ethics.

39   "Code of Ethics and Standards of Conduct," CFP
      Board, October 1, 2019, https://www.cfp.net/ethics/
      code-of-ethics-and-standards-of-conduct.

Chapter 6: Buy-and-Hold Pie Chart Promoters

40   Edwin J. Elton and Martin J. Gruber, "Risk Reduction and
      Portfolio Size: An Analytic Solution," *Journal of Business*
      50, no. 4 (October 1977): 415–37, https://pages.stern.nyu.
      edu/~eelton/papers/77-oct.pdf.

41   A fee-based investment advisor is a financial professional who charges clients fees for their advisory services—such as a percentage of assets under management (AUM), flat fees, hourly rates, or retainers—but may also receive commissions from selling specific financial products or investment vehicles. This compensation structure distinguishes them from both commission-only advisors (who are paid solely by product providers) and fee-only advisors (who are paid exclusively by clients and never receive commissions). See Julia Kagan, "Fee-Based Investment: What It Is, How It Works, Example," Investopedia, August 15, 2024, https://www.investopedia.com/terms/f/feebasedinvestment.asp.

Chapter 7: Portfolio Management? I Think Not!

42   According to the CMT Association, "Tom Dorsey is the Co-Founder & Chief Executive Officer of Dorsey, Wright & Associates, a registered investment advisory firm that provides quality equity analysis and options strategies to member firms and institutions. . . . Dorsey has become one of the industry's foremost experts in Point and Figure Charting and teaches this method worldwide." "Tom Dorsey," CMT Association, accessed September 2, 2025, https://cmtassociation.org/presenter/tom-dorsey.

43   "How to Create Candlestick Charts," InetSoft, accessed September 2, 2025, https://www.inetsoft.com/info/how-to-create-candlestick-charts.

44   TC2000® (TC2000.com) combines charting, stock and
      option screening, and trading features in an easy-to-use,
      polished platform. It has been recognized as an industry
      leader for over twenty-five years (as the name of the
      company hints). Many thanks to TC2000 for allowing me
      to use its outstanding charts in the pages of this book. The
      company is a class act with a superior charting product.

45   This took effect on July 30, 2009. See "Fitch Withdraws
      Chevy Chase Bank, F.S.B. Ratings Upon Assumption by
      Capital One, N.A.," Fitch Ratings, July 31, 2009, https://
      www.fitchratings.com/research/banks/fitch-withdraws-
      chevy-chase-bank-fsb-ratings-upon-assumption-by-
      capital-one-na-31-07-2009.

46   Sarah Butcher, "How Attractive Must You Be to
      Work in Banking?," eFinancialCareers, July 24, 2015,
      https://www.efinancialcareers.com/news/2015/07/
      how-attractive-must-you-be-to-work-in-banking.

47   Katie Little, "The Most Attractive Bankers Are…," CNBC,
      July 30, 2014, www.cnbc.com/2014/07/29/the-most-
      attractive-bankers-are.html.

48   Owen Hargie, David Dickson, and Dennis Tourish,
      Communication Skills for Effective Management (Palgrave
      McMillan, 2004), https://26202235.s21i.faiusr.com/61/
      ABUIABA9GAAgobKs-wUoivSDiAE.pdf.

Chapter 8: The Biggest White-Collar Scam

49   Ben Geier, "Financial Advisor Fees: Fee-Only vs. Fee-
      Based," SmartAsset, July 11, 2025, https://smartasset.com/
      financial-advisor/fee-based-vs-fee-only-financial-advisor.

Chapter 9: Why I Had to Write This Book

50   *Britannica*, "McCarthyism," by Paul J. Achter, last updated
      August 25, 2025, https://www.britannica.com/event/
      McCarthyism.

51   Jeffrey Sandler, "Evaluating the Performance of Jim
      Cramer's Stock Picks" (thesis, Schreyer Honors College,
      Pennsylvania State University, 2013), https://honors.
      libraries.psu.edu/files/final_submissions/1831.

52   Steve LeCompte, "Jim Cramer Deconstructed," CXO
      Advisory Group, June 15, 2009, https://www.cxoadvisory.
      com/individual-gurus/jim-cramer.

53   Nadya Josifov, "How Good Are Jim Cramer's Stock
      Picks?," AskMoney, May 20, 2025, www.askmoney.com/
      investing/jim-cramers-stock-picks.

Chapter 10: A Little Math to Scare You

54   Chart as of close of business, July 14, 2025.

55   Ye Xie, Liz Capo McCormick, and Joel Leon, "Long-
      Bond Revolt Pressures 60/40 Comeback in Chaotic
      2025 Market," *Bloomberg*, May 25, 2025, https://www.
      bloomberg.com/news/articles/2025-05-25/long-bond-
      revolt-pressures-60-40-comeback-in-chaotic-2025-market.

Chapter 11: Insanity, Doubled

56   Ali Hibbs, "Sanctuary Snags Florida-Based UBS Team
      Managing $2 Billion," *AdvisorHub*, May 12, 2025, https://
      www.advisorhub.com/sanctuary-snags-florida-based-ubs-
      team-managing-2-billion.

PART THREE: YOU EAT THE BEAR
Chapter 12: Data-Driven, Data-Proven Statements

57   Ed Prince, "What the Wealthiest Clients Really Want," Rethinking65, March 4, 2024, https://rethinking65.com/what-the-wealthiest-clients-really-want.

58   Periodic and total return calculators and methodology of our historical stock market. See PK, "S&P 500 Return Calculator, with Dividend Reinvestment," DQYDJ, August 31, 2025, https://dqydj.com/sp-500-return-calculator; Cory Mitchell, "Historical Average Stock Market Returns for S&P 500 (5-year to 150-year averages)," TradeThatSwing, June 12, 2025, https://tradethatswing.com/average-historical-stock-market-returns-for-sp-500-5-year-up-to-150-year-averages; PK, "S&P 500 Periodic Reinvestment Calculator (With Dividends)," DQYDJ, accessed September 2, 2025, https://dqydj.com/sp-500-periodic-reinvestment-calculator-dividends; and *S&P 500 Carry Adjusted Total Return Index Methodology* (S&P Dow Jones Indices, 2025), https://www.spglobal.com/spdji/en/documents/methodologies/methodology-sp-500-carry-adjusted-total-return-index.pdf.

59   "QQQ,BRK-A: Total Return Chart (with Dividends Reinvested)," Total Real Returns, accessed June 13, 2025, https://totalrealreturns.com/n/QQQ,BRK-A.

60 "VOO: Total Return Chart (with Dividends Reinvested),"
    Total Real Returns, accessed June 13, 2025, https://
    totalrealreturns.com/n/VOO.

Chapter 14: Take Your Wealth Away from the Pie Chart Promoters

61 "Man Struck, Killed by Metro Train at Shady
    Grove. Witnesses Say Man Was on Tracks
    Intentionally," NBC4 Washington, December
    19, 2008, https://www.nbcwashington.com/local/
    person-struck-by-metro-train-at-shady-grove/1847570.

PART FOUR: THIS MATH CAGES THE BEAR
Chapter 15: The Eleven Charts

62 All eleven of these charts plus the MAGS chart show their
    status as of close of business, Thursday, July 3, 2025, 4:00
    p.m. EST, except the first three which are as of close of
    business July 14, 2025. In other words, they all represent a
    YTD status, from January 1 to July 13 or 14, 2025. These
    charts are provided by TC2000®.

63 "Morningstar™ Style Box," Morningstar, 2009, https://
    www.morningstar.com/content/dam/marketing/apac/au/
    pdfs/Legal/Stylebox_Factsheet.pdf.

Chapter 16: Ten Best, Ten Worst Days

64 Thune, "2025 Teaches the Wisdom of Buy and Hold
    Investing."

Chapter 17: The Truth About Variable Universal Life

65 Nancy Rooney and Serena DiBianco, "Portfolio Resilience: Ways to Strengthen a Portfolio—Especially for Unpredictable Markets," J.P. Morgan Private Bank, March 28, 2025 https://privatebank.jpmorgan.com/eur/en/insights/markets-and-investing/ways-to-strengthen-a-portfolio-especially-for-unpredictable-markets.

66 James H. Hunt, *Variable Universal Life Insurance: Is It Worth It?* (Consumer Federation of America, 2003), https://consumerfed.org/pdfs/VULReport0203.pdf.

67 "American Express Financial Advisors (Now Known as Ameriprise Financial Services, Inc.) to Pay $30 Million to Settle Revenue Sharing Charges," US Securities and Exchange Commission, December 1, 2005, https://www.sec.gov/news/press/2005-168.htm.

68 Associated Press, "American Express to Spin Off Advisory Unit: The Financial Services Giant American Express Co. Said Tuesday It Plans to Spin Off Its Financial Advisory Business to Its Shareholders and Focus on Its Charge and Credit Card, Payments Processing, and Travel Businesses," NBC News, February 1, 2005, https://www.nbcnews.com/id/wbna6894174.

69 "American Express Is Fined for Improper Annuity Sales," *The Wall Street Journal*, December 4, 2002, https://www.wsj.com/articles/SB103902133357737353.

70   The MEC corridor is the required difference between the policy's death benefit and its cash value. The term *non-MEC corridor* refers to a key requirement that allows a life insurance policy to retain its non-MEC status and thereby maintain favorable tax treatment. Non-MEC policies maintain tax benefits such as allowing tax-free loans and withdrawals up to the policy's cost basis. See Mark P. Cussen, "Avoiding the Modified Endowment Contract Trap," Investopedia, August 1, 2023, https://www.investopedia.com/articles/insurance/10/avoid-modified-endowment-contract-traps.asp; and 26 U.S. Code § 7702A – Modified Endowment Contract Defined.

71   Mark P. Cussen, "What Are Financial Securities Licenses?," Investopedia, November 22, 2024, https://www.investopedia.com/articles/financialcareers/07/securities_licenses.asp.

72   I was a minority owner of Keystone Capital Management (KCM). I was also its largest producer, managing the VA/VUL products. The company was owned by Charlton Jones, one of the smartest men ever alive. We would still be working together, but he died of cancer in 2009 and I had to bring all management services in-house.

73   Julia Kagan, "Understanding 1035 Exchanges: Tax-Free Insurance and Annuity Transfers," Investopedia, August 8, 2025, https://www.investopedia.com/terms/s/sec1035ex.asp.

74   See my firm's website for more information about how we work: https://www.rfsadvisors.com/our-approach.